ESSEX VILLAINS

ROGUES, RASCALS AND REPROBATES

PAUL WREYFORD

The History Press

This book is dedicated to Glen and Emmeline
– my own adorable 'little rascals'.

First published 2012

The History Press
The Mill, Brimscombe Port
Stroud, Gloucestershire, GL5 2QG
www.thehistorypress.co.uk

British Library Cataloguing in Publication Data.
A catalogue record for this book is available from the British Library.

ISBN 978 0 7524 6574 6

Typesetting and origination by The History Press
Printed in Great Britain

Contents

Acknowledgements

I would like to thank all those that have aided my research in some way, with particular thanks to Epping Forest District Museum, Colchester Castle Museum and the Essex Record Office. All photographs featured in the book have been taken by me.

Introduction

Every county in England has had its rogues, rascals and reprobates over the years – and yet, Essex has perhaps had more than its fair share of them. Even today it is a county with a reputation, though the much-maligned Essex boy and girl are saints compared to some of the sinners that came before them.

Essex can boast (or perhaps rue) a diverse range of villains. Bordering the capital, the county has played an important role in many political events, a number of rebels having plotted and even took up arms against Parliament or the monarchy within its boundaries. And many travellers on their way to and from London had to pass through vast Epping Forest, the stomping ground of highwaymen such as Dick Turpin – perhaps the county's most famous bad guy.

Despite its proximity to the capital, Essex has more shoreline than most counties in England. Smuggling was a big business and sometimes almost every inhabitant of a village was at it. Essex was – and still is – known as a witch county too. However, the man responsible for bringing witches to justice – the notorious Matthew Hopkins – was perhaps the biggest villain of them all.

Even royalty – who have used the county as a rural escape for centuries – have been more than roguish in their behaviour over the years; adultery and even murder being among their transgressions. Other notable persons of high standing have conspired or cheated to get to the top.

Not all villains in this book actually lived in Essex, but all knew it well or carried out their villainous acts within its boundaries. This is obviously not an exhaustive list of rogues, rascals and reprobates. There have, of course, been far too many. It is just a selection, concentrating on some of the more infamous or interesting bad guys.

It has to be said that sometimes things are not always black and white. Even some of our notorious miscreants may not have been as bad as they have been painted over the years. On the other hand, some of our so-called heroes had a dark side and might not have been as holy as our history books have portrayed them; time has a habit of distorting the truth. While every effort has been made to ensure the facts in this book are correct, one has to admit some of the villains included have become legends, and their lives – often romanticised by scribes over the years – may indeed now resemble something closer to fiction than fact.

One can only apologise to the 'villains' who might have felt aggrieved at being included in this book – and to those who might have been disappointed to be omitted!

Paul Wreyford, 2012

Chapter One

Highwaymen

'Stand and deliver!'

You would not have wanted to hear those words outside your coach on a dark night. Travelling by road to and from London – in particular through Epping Forest – was once a risky business, but a profitable one for highwaymen. No traveller was safe. Even King William III was a victim of a gang of ruffians on one occasion.

Epping Forest was not the only haunt of highwaymen, but it became notorious for those preying on wealthy but vulnerable travellers. It was also home to the most famous bandit of them all.

Dick Turpin

Dick Turpin can stake a claim to being one of the most famous villains the country has ever produced. He is certainly Essex's pride and joy when it comes to all things bad.

Turpin was not just a highwayman – though that is the trade he is most associated with – but he was also a poacher, thief, burglar and even murderer. His name is synonymous with villainy, though time has been kind to him, the Dick Turpin most know today being a romantic figure in the style of Robin Hood. However, Turpin did not rob from the poor to give to the rich. He stole whatever and from whomever he could, terrorising residents and travellers in and around Epping Forest, which was to Turpin what Sherwood Forest was to Robin Hood.

Richard Turpin was born at what is now the Bluebell Inn, Hempstead, near Saffron Walden, at the beginning of the eighteenth century. He was the son of the innkeeper, a former butcher. He followed in the footsteps of his father, becoming an apprentice butcher in east London, but was dismissed due to his improper behaviour. However, Turpin soon put his new-found butchery skills to good use after discovering that selling meat obtained with his own hands was far more profitable than purchasing it from a farmer. He targeted the cattle of his neighbours, though this might not have been the best idea. According to one account, after stealing two oxen from Plaistow, Turpin was followed home by two of the victim's servants. Even with two carcasses hanging up in the Turpin abode, more proof was required that these were the two animals from Plaistow. A warrant for Turpin's arrest was only issued after it was discovered that he disposed of hides

The Bluebell Inn, Essex – Dick Turpin's birthplace.

The plaque on the wall of the Bluebell Inn commemorating Dick Turpin's birthplace.

at nearby Waltham Abbey, where two oxen skins were subsequently discovered. It is believed Turpin evaded capture by escaping through a back window of his house when the law came to call. It was a significant moment, as it was to lead to a life on the run.

Turpin went into hiding and eventually joined the Gregory Gang (also known as the Essex Gang) – a band of poachers and rustlers whose chief place of work was Epping Forest and London. It has to be remembered that the forest was even bigger than it is now. It was the perfect hideaway and also rich with venison.

However, poaching deer was not as profitable as Turpin and his colleagues would have liked. Not content to just target helpless animals, the outlaws turned their attention to vulnerable humans. Breaking into isolated homes throughout the forest proved to be even easier and far more rewarding.

Turpin was not an amenable man, and appears to have had few morals or a conscience. One successful burglary took place at Loughton, in 1735, and highlighted the gang's cruel methods. The elderly resident was told she would be held over her roaring fire until she revealed where her life savings were hidden. Turpin showed little remorse in robbing a vulnerable member of society, and took to the bottle to celebrate a very profitable day's work. It is said he got so drunk that he failed to turn up to the gang's next job!

Force was often used on people in their own homes, and it was not long before a reward was offered for the capture of Turpin and his fellow outlaws. Most of the gang were eventually apprehended and either jailed or hanged.

It is believed at this point, that Turpin took another road on his way to the gallows – in more ways than one. He took to terrorising the highway, robbing travellers at gunpoint, and, in doing so, earning his reputation as one of Britain's most famous criminals.

Life on the road also led Turpin to Matthew 'Tom' King, his most famous partner in crime, who was known as the 'Gentleman Highwayman'. King was also a notable 'celebrity', but, according to legend, Turpin obviously did not recognise him when he tried to rob him one day. Believing King to be just another wealthy gentleman on his way through the forest, Turpin stopped King's horse and produced a gun – demanding the contents of his purse. King certainly knew Turpin and is said to have declared, 'What is this, dog eat dog?' He invited the young outlaw to join his gang and Turpin accepted.

Further robberies enhanced the reputations of King and Turpin. Travellers on the Cambridge to London road were forced to carry firearms themselves, fearful of being apprehended by the outlaws.

The gang were based at the heart of Epping Forest, and famously took shelter in a cave in the High Beach area. Bushes and bracken camouflaged the secret hiding place, but while the outlaws remained unobserved, they themselves still had a good view of the road and any unwary traveller. Turpin's wife is said to have brought the gang supplies and even resided in the cave herself on occasions.

The road through Epping Forest was once a very treacherous route to take.

It was not long before Turpin was wanted for murder too. A servant to one of the keepers of Epping Forest – despite the gang's ever-growing reputation – was presumably lured by the reward offered for the capture of Turpin. Some say Turpin at first mistook Thomas Morris for a poacher when he approached him with a gun, but Morris had come for more than rabbits. The highwayman shot the servant dead.

It was not the only time Turpin killed a man, according to some. At about the same time, he is believed to have been responsible for the death of his partner-in-crime King too. 'Captain' King, as he was sometimes known, may have escaped with his life when the two highwaymen first met, but it was a bullet supposedly fired by his friend that eventually did for him.

It all started when a traveller was robbed of his racehorse. After his ordeal, the victim raised the alarm, not prepared to let the highwaymen get away with it. Wanted posters were put up throughout London and Essex.

The newly-acquired horse, which some say Turpin named Black Bess, was later spotted outside a tavern in Whitechapel. The landlord of the establishment apprehended King's brother who had come to collect it. The sibling of King was told that he would be set free if he 'shopped' the real culprits and he duly obliged, revealing that his brother was waiting for the horse close by. Matthew King was confronted and reached for his gun, but it did not fire. Meanwhile, Turpin had been watching from a safe distance and rode to the rescue – or Matthew King certainly must have thought that was what he was doing. He shouted to Turpin to shoot their apprehender. Turpin did fire his gun, but the bullet hit Matthew King, and Turpin fled the scene. King did not die instantly and, in fact, lived on for about a week, which was enough time to inform the authorities where Turpin was hiding, but, of course, the elusive highwayman had long gone before they paid him a visit.

Most assume Turpin shot his ally and friend by accident, and he apparently lamented his actions afterwards, but others claim he may have killed King in cold blood, perhaps in an attempt to stop him talking. Other historians are of the opinion it was not even Turpin who fired the fateful shot.

The incident marked the end of Turpin's reign in Epping Forest. Fearing the game would soon be up for him too, he decided to make a clean break and moved up north to start a new life of crime. He eventually settled in Yorkshire and took on the guise of a gentleman horse dealer named John Palmer. He accompanied fellow gentlemen on shooting parties, and all were oblivious to his real identity and past misdemeanours. They were also unaware he was stealing their horses. It is said that he even resold horses to those he had stolen them from!

The beginning of his end was perhaps, typically, self-inflicted. On returning from a day out with his newfound friends, the rash Turpin needlessly shot a fowl. When he was reprimanded by a labourer, Palmer threatened to shoot him too. A warrant was issued for his arrest.

The authorities soon discovered other crimes committed by the accused were more severe. Turpin might have gone to the gallows as just another highwayman and horse stealer operating in the counties of Lincolnshire and Yorkshire, as his real identity had not yet been discovered. The execution of 'John Palmer' would have probably barely raised an eyebrow.

It was the cost of a 'stamp' that ensured Dick Turpin would have the send-off he perhaps deserved. While in prison in York, Turpin wrote to his brother-in-law at Hempstead. The letter was returned to the post office unopened, as it appears the brother-in-law, for whatever reason, refused to pay the delivery charge. The letter fell into the hands of a schoolmaster who had taught Turpin to write. He recognised the handwriting and took it to the law. And so, John Palmer was revealed to be the notorious Dick Turpin.

People from all over flocked to York Castle to get a glimpse of the condemned man, though there are some even now who doubt Palmer was Epping Forest's – and England's – most wanted outlaw.

Turpin remained true to his character until the last. He even apparently mocked his own fate, hiring personal mourners for his execution. And so, in 1739, Dick Turpin was put into a cart, his mourners in tow, and driven to the gallows. Still seemingly indifferent to his destiny, he is said to have bowed to the crowds before his short, but eventful, life of crime was ended.

Swift Nicks

Author Daniel Defoe was of the opinion that Swift Nicks – and not Dick Turpin and Black Bess – made the legendary 'non-stop' ride from London to York. The incredible feat of endurance was

The World's End pub, in the shadow of Tilbury Fort and Tilbury power station, was once the haunt of highwayman Swift Nicks.

accredited to Turpin for many years, but there is no evidence to suggest he made that journey in so short a time.

Defoe, writing in *A Tour Through the Whole Island of Great Britain*, attributes the ride to a man named Swift Nicks, of whom little is known. It took place in 1676 – long before Turpin was even born. The author said that the bandit committed a robbery in Kent in the early hours of the morning. Making his escape, he took the ferry across the Thames to Tilbury and rode through Essex, briefly stopping at Chelmsford to refresh. He arrived in York that evening. The idea was to establish an alibi – and it worked. He made sure he was noticed, talking to none other than the Lord Mayor of York while watching a game of bowls. Indeed, when Swift Nicks was accused of the crime and the case came to court, he was acquitted. It was said he could not possibly have committed the robbery being so far away in Yorkshire. Defoe said it was the King of England himself – Charles II – who gave the thief his nickname.

The identity of Swift Nicks has never been discovered. Most claim he was John Nevison – a Yorkshire highwayman who was executed in 1684. The outlaw is believed to have known at least a bit of Essex, however. It is said he frequented the World's End pub next to Tilbury Fort – it being so close to the ferry – though it is unlikely he would have had much time for even a quick half on that memorable day in 1676. He must have liked a tipple there, however, as his ghost was also said to reside at the riverside establishment for many years following his death.

Defoe himself – who set the beginning of his novel *Moll Flanders* in Colchester – lived for a spell at Tilbury, so may have learned of the tale of Swift Nicks during that time.

Cutter Lynch

A good disguise was important to the average highwayman. Some led respectable lives by day, and neighbours were oblivious to what they got up to after dark. It was important they or – in the case of Jerry 'Cutter' Lynch – their horse were never identified. This is where Lynch, a notorious highwayman of Leigh-on-Sea, had a problem. While he himself may not have stood out in the crowd, Brown Meg – his trusty mare – certainly did, as she did not have any ears! It meant Lynch had to make some false ones

The people of Leigh-on-Sea were blissfully unaware new neighbour Gilbert Craddock was a notorious highwayman.

in order that he would not be identified because of his steed's conspicuous abnormality.

Lynch, whose real name was Gilbert Craddock, was a respectable London businessman by day. He was educated and a gentleman – or so people thought. Not long before his death in the mid-eighteenth century, Lynch bought Leigh Park House, which was almost a ruin at the time. He and Brown Meg stayed at the Smack Inn on the waterside while renovating the property. His new home became known as Lapwater Hall. It is said the builders wanted more than the set number of pots of ale they had been provided with, prompting Lynch – anxious for the work to be completed as soon as possible – to respond with the suggestion that they should 'lap water' from the horse pond if they were thirsty.

Ironically, the same pond was to play a big part in the death of Lynch. His body was discovered in it after officers of the law had given chase. The highwayman was wounded as he tried to escape the authorities. He had managed to get back to Lapwater Hall and, as his pursuers reached his property, had seemingly evaded capture by creeping out of the back of the house. Presumably, officers thought he had given them the slip and gave up the chase, as he was not discovered until the following day. It is believed Lynch had either hidden in the pond or fallen in, his wound preventing him from climbing out of the water. It was said Brown Meg was found close by, along with a pair of wax horse ears.

Sixteen-String Jack

Not all highwaymen kept a low profile. While the likes of Cutter Lynch took pains not to be noticed, Sixteen-String Jack – such was his audacity – deliberately drew attention to himself. He gained his nickname because of his unusual attire, notably the eight coloured tassels that dangled from both knees of his breeches. He wore stylish waistcoats and ruffled shirts, while also donning hats covered with buttons and ribbons. The clothes were as flamboyant as the man that wore them.

The real name of this eccentric of the road was John Rann. He was another to operate in Epping Forest and there is now a pub at Theydon Bois, named in his honour. Rann is believed to have started to don extravagant clothes while working as a coachman to wealthy gentlemen. He probably aspired to be like them, but – realising he would not achieve his goal in this way – eventually became a pickpocket. Even that was probably not as profitable as he would have liked, and he soon realised even more money could be made as a highwayman. Rann operated all over London and not just in Epping Forest. He would openly boast about his life as an outlaw. On one occasion, he is said to have pushed himself to the front of the crowd watching an execution and boldly declared he would one day be the main participant. He was right; Rann was just 24 when he was hanged at Tyburn in 1774.

Despite his outlandish appearance, Rann proved to be hard to get as far as the authorities were concerned. He was accused of various crimes on at least six occasions, but was acquitted each time. As well as being a natty dresser, Rann was a smart talker as well. He is believed to have escaped the gallows on so many occasions because of his guile and brazenness. One of his great escapes came in the same year as his death. Rann was before the famous Bow Street magistrate Sir John Fielding and, when asked

The Sixteen–String Jack pub in Theydon Bois.

The fate of Sixteen-String Jack is made abundantly clear on the pub's sign.

whether he had anything to say in his defence, the highwayman coolly replied, 'I know no more of the matter than you do, nor half so much neither.' After hours of questioning, Rann, sporting coloured bows in his leg irons and a bundle of flowers fixed to the breast of his coat, was freed.

However, the end of Sixteen-String Jack was not long in coming. Rann was arrested after robbing the chaplain of Princess Amelia. This time he could not talk himself free.

Perhaps unsurprisingly, Rann was brash and seemingly fearless to the end. While awaiting his fate in prison, he is said to have dined in his cell with seven pretty ladies on one occasion, the party going on well into the night.

Even on the day of his execution, this colourful highwayman reputedly showed no remorse or apparent fear, accepting his fate with an air of indifference. Some claimed he even cheerfully swapped banter with the onlookers and danced a jig on the scaffold. It was almost as if Sixteen-String Jack believed his meeting with the hangman's noose was inevitable – the natural finale to an eventful and theatrical life.

Chapter Two

Smugglers

Essex has more coastline than the average county in England. Low-lying, blessed with many tributaries and hidden creeks, it is perhaps the perfect location for landing illegal cargo.

For many remote villages, smuggling became a way of life – and death. Author Sabine Baring-Gould, in his novel *Mehalah*, suggested smugglers could be brutes that stopped at nothing. He spoke of a boatload of revenue men who had their throats cut at Sunken Island, and were then buried beneath their upturned vessel in a local churchyard, reputedly at Salcott-cum-Virley – not too far from the writer's own home on Mersea Island.

Many ordinary and even respected pillars of the community were also involved in the 'free trade', including clergymen who often allowed booty to be stored in the church vestry. In the isolated village of Paglesham – surely once the home of smuggling in Essex – it was said the entire community was involved in some way. It was reputed so much gin was landed, locals used it to clean their windows! It is in Paglesham where we find the most famous of all Essex smugglers, a man that did his best to live up to the romantic notion many still have of a smuggler.

William 'Hard Apple' Blyth

Paglesham was once a smuggling hotspot, as the village sign highlights.

It is perhaps ironic that William Blyth – often labelled the king of the smugglers in Essex – was never actually charged with any smuggling. The romantic would probably say that was because of his guile and skill at evading the customs officers, though others have suggested his many amazing exploits were more fiction than fact.

What we know about 'Hard Apple', a nickname presumably relating to his strong head for alcohol, is pretty much down to one man – local magistrate John Harriott, of Broomhills, Great Stambridge, near Rochford. The escapades of Blyth emanated from Harriott's memoirs *Struggles through Life*, which were published in the early part of the nineteenth century. The work sealed Blyth's notoriety.

Harriott had many tales to tell of Blyth, his near neighbour, and particularly focused on the way he eluded the authorities. On one occasion, according to Harriott, Blyth did fall into the hands of the customs men. A revenue vessel had apprehended the smuggler and his crew, and the game looked up for them. However, Blyth reportedly used his drinking prowess and powers of persuasion to good effect. It is said that, while the authorities removed the smuggled goods from the boat, Blyth set about negotiating as to exactly how many tubs of spirit should be seized from his vessel. The bargaining took place over a heavy drinking session and ended with the revenue men becoming a little tipsy to say the least. At the end of it all, Blyth was able to transfer the removed smuggled goods back to his boat and was also said to have gained some extra booty that had been on the revenue cutter at the time!

William 'Hard Apple' Blyth often frequented the Punch Bowl pub at Paglesham.

The sign for the Punch Bowl pub.

On another occasion, customs officers apprehended Blyth while he was operating just off the French coast. On the journey back to England, the cutter – with Blyth now a prisoner onboard – ran aground. The desperate crew persuaded Blyth to use his considerable knowledge and experience of tides to steer the stricken vessel off the sands. There was a catch for the authorities, however. In return for this service, Blyth was promised his freedom.

Often the revenue officers were more concerned in retrieving the smuggled

Broomhills was the former home of magistrate John Harriott.

goods than putting the men responsible behind bars. Many turned a blind eye towards the perpetrators in order to avoid a lengthy court case, and some customs men were even said to be in league with the smugglers.

Even magistrate Harriott – who later founded the Thames River Police – used the smugglers to his advantage in 1786. He tells of an occasion he drank with smugglers, and then hitched a lift home with Blyth and his Paglesham colleagues.

Harriott had concluded business on the Continent and was in need of a quick passage back to England. He knew the habits of the Paglesham smugglers, and the fact they frequented a particular inn at Dunkirk. When he arrived in the evening, he met some Kent smugglers who informed him that Blyth would be arriving later that night. To pass away the time, Harriott had a drink or two with those already there, taking care not to reveal his true identity. And so, the evening was spent drinking toasts. It appears Harriott did have some scruples, however. He refused to join in the toast declaring damnation to all revenue laws and officers. Instead, he convinced his fellow drinkers to change the toast to 'revenue laws and officers forever'! Harriott had rightly pointed out that, without the revenue laws and officers, there would be no smuggling, and the present company would be much the poorer for it.

Despite his reputation, little is known about the life of Blyth. It is thought he was an oyster merchant, which would also account for his trips across the Channel. The fact he was also later a grocer, churchwarden and member of the parish council, backs up the theory that Harriott may have been a little too liberal with the truth when penning his memoirs. However, many respectable people were often tempted into smuggling and some like the idea that, as village grocer, no record of Blyth's crimes is available for the simple fact that he used pages torn out of the parish register to wrap up smuggled bacon. And whether truth or fiction, stories of Blyth fighting and defeating a bull with his bare hands – and having a fondness for eating the glass after he had downed his drink – do add to the romanticism of it all. It is characters like 'Hard Apple' Blyth who have given smuggling its romantic image, where in truth it was a nasty business and many innocent people lost their lives because of it.

Blyth died an old man in 1830, and was buried in the churchyard at Paglesham, close to the Punch Bowl pub – his

Remote Paglesham was ideal for smugglers.

favourite drinking hole. His reputation lives on and he is even depicted on the village sign, a fitting tribute to the so-called – and perhaps worthy – king of the smugglers.

Philip Sainty

Sainty by name, but not saintly by nature. This famous son of Wivenhoe is a classic example of how even respectable figures were often tempted into the murky world of the smugglers. However, Philip Sainty – thanks to his own special talent and the generosity of a wealthy 'benefactor' – managed to redeem himself and gain lasting fame for something other than his illegal dealings on the coast.

The gravestone of Sainty, which can be found in the parish churchyard at Wivenhoe, informs the reader that the deceased was the builder of the Marquess of Anglesey's yacht *Pearl*. The *Pearl* was one of the finest vessels in the country at the time. Sainty built it at Wivenhoe in about 1820. The yacht was manned by a local crew and skippered by William Ham, another resident of the town. It was the start of a long and famous tradition on the Colne Estuary for skippering and crewing racing yachts. Henry William Paget, the first Marquess of Anglesey, commissioned Sainty to build it – but he first had to get him out of jail. Sainty was in prison for smuggling at the time. Not that this would stop the Marquess getting his own way. He is reportedly to have declared, 'Even if he (Sainty) were in Hell, I would have him out.' And the Marquess did – though it is not known how he secured Sainty's release, whether it was by using his political influence or putting his hand into his pocket.

Sainty certainly had a reputation as a fine boatbuilder, but most of his luggers up to then had been built for those involved in the smuggling trade. His vessels often got the better of the pursuing customs officers, earning Sainty his reputation as a skilled craftsman.

The Marquess was a distinguished statesman and soldier. He returned from the Battle of Waterloo a hero, having lost a leg in action. Now with more time to pursue his love of sailing, the Marquess decided Sainty was the man for the job of building his latest yacht.

Riverside Wivenhoe was the home and final resting place of smuggler and boatbuilder Philip Sainty.

The grave of Philip Sainty.

Sainty was not the only boatbuilder to turn to smuggling to make a quick buck. He had fallen on difficult times and knew, through experience, what it was like to be bankrupt. Perhaps it was no surprise he should view smuggling as the answer to his problems. The activity was rife and almost everyone was at it. Sainty's brother was also a part-time smuggler.

As well as building boats for smugglers, Sainty made a number of runs to the Continent himself – mostly for casks of spirits at the order of a local publican. The determination of the Marquess to get his man was a godsend for Sainty, as his release and commission to build the *Pearl* transformed his life. It is said Sainty agreed to give up smuggling as one of the conditions of his release. He became a celebrated designer and builder of fine yachts. His past misdemeanours were soon forgotten and he became a respectable citizen once more, now building boats for the wealthy, rather than for the smuggling trade.

Ironically, Sainty even gave the revenue men a helping hand in the fight against smuggling. Such was his reputation for building brilliant boats, they actually asked him to build some for them!

Saucy Jack

Few lived up to the stereotypical image of a smuggler. In reality, most in the trade were brutish or very ordinary. One exception was John Skinner, better known as Saucy Jack.

Skinner was a ladies man and cut a dashing figure, a real charmer who left numerous women heartbroken. He was the Don Juan of smugglers. It is thought he lured many a wife from their husband before breaking their hearts.

Skinner led a life of debauchery. He was presumably only intent on satisfying his own needs, often at the expense of others, including his own wife. His love of money ultimately led to his downfall.

Brightlingsea-born smuggler Saucy Jack would have known the Colne Estuary very well.

Skinner was born in Brightlingsea in the early eighteenth century. His middle-class upbringing, with a good education, offered him a head start in life. His marriage to a wealthy Essex woman, of which a substantial fortune came attached, would have made him the envy of many. However, the money soon started to disappear faster than it was coming in. Skinner had three loves: drink, gambling and women. While he squandered the family fortune in brothels and gambling dens, his poor wife suffered. It was not long before Skinner had blown his wife's fortune and was unable to pay his mounting debts. This selfish rake, rather than being full of remorse, abandoned the woman he married and she ended up in the parish workhouse. Even when Skinner prospered in subsequent years, it is said he never sent her a penny.

It was when Skinner left London to run the King's Head – a Romford inn – that his fortunes changed. It was here Skinner discovered the lucrative business of smuggling. He was not the only publican to turn to smuggled alcohol as a way of increasing their profits.

Skinner became one of the most notorious smugglers in the county, though it is not really known what part he played in the business. What is known is that he certainly profited from it. And he soon discovered that far bigger profits could be made in smuggling than by pulling pints. He eventually gave up his Romford hostelry and moved to the outskirts of Colchester, where he ran two farms, purely as a decoy for his main business activities – smuggling.

The beginning of the end for Skinner came when he fell out with one of his servants, a man named Brett, who is thought to have betrayed him. The hot-tempered Skinner flew into a rage on discovering the betrayal and shot Brett at close range. When the red mist cleared, Skinner may have felt some pangs of remorse, for he went to see a surgeon in Colchester, informing him that a man had been shot and needed urgent treatment. The surgeon came to Skinner's house and did all he could for the unfortunate Brett. In fact, the dying servant survived the night, but died the next day.

It is thought that Brett, perhaps in loyalty to his master or because he was too weak, never actually revealed who gave him the wound, but few had any doubt who fired the fateful shot. When the authorities came to arrest Skinner, he was gone. It is assumed he fled the area and lived in hiding for the next couple of years.

Skinner might have got away with his crime, but the lure of more money sealed his fate. Probably through friends, the smuggler-cum-murderer discovered that – some two years after going into hiding – he had come into property. There was a catch, however. To take possession of his estate, Skinner would have to come out of hiding and personally attend a copyhold court. He did just that. Presumably, Skinner thought the passage of time would come to his rescue and, without fear, he casually walked into court to claim his inheritance. He was instantly recognised and arrested.

Skinner spent his final days in Chelmsford Gaol. He dreaded the shame of facing his fate in front of a crowd and tried to kill himself with a knife. It was presumably smuggled into the jail. It appears he was a brilliant smuggler to the last! Half-dead, he was hauled to the scaffold in 1746 and executed.

The body of Skinner was taken back to Brightlingsea, and buried in the parish churchyard. An anonymous tract, written after his death, described Saucy Jack 'as great a smuggler as any' in Essex.

Elizabeth Little

Smuggling was not an occupation exclusive to men. One of the most successful 'traders' in Essex was Elizabeth Little. She ran a shop in Leigh-on-Sea, in the mid-nineteenth century. Her property had a secret underground room with direct access to the waterside, and one can reasonably assume her stock – consisting of the finest silks, lace, perfume and even gin – was not always obtained from the local wholesaler! Leigh, like many coastal locations, was a hotbed for smuggling, and Elizabeth was probably one of many retailers tempted to increase their profits by illegal means.

Elizabeth was certainly a respected member of the community, and a woman of good education. She was renowned for her lavish dinner parties, which consisted of the best food, wine and conversation to be had in town. She was every bit the lady in public, but presumably possessed a sense of adventure and liked nothing better than getting her hands dirty in order to help fund the lifestyle she had become accustomed to. It is not really known what role she played in the trading of illicit goods. Her brothers

Even today it is not difficult to imagine the likes of Elizabeth Little unloading smuggled goods at quaint Leigh-on-Sea.

probably did most of the runs to the Continent, but, while they may have provided the brawn, Elizabeth certainly provided the brains. It is thought she was the organiser of the whole operation.

Elizabeth certainly knew how to handle a boat and seemingly possessed a fine knowledge of all things maritime, including local tides. That is evident from one memorable escape from the clutches of the authorities. A coastguard cutter was lying in wait when Elizabeth and her brothers reached the mouth of the Thames, close to Shoeburyness, on their way home from a successful operation. As the family tried to make a run for it, the coastguards gave chase and opened fire on their vessel. One of Elizabeth's brothers was wounded and – in a desperate attempt to elude the pursuers – she steered their boat inland towards Barling Creek – a tributary of the River Roach – fully aware the cutter could not follow in shallow waters. However, fearing they would themselves be stranded at low tide and become sitting ducks, Elizabeth decided to continue overland and ordered another of her brothers to take their empty boat back home, under the very noses of the coastguards. An undertaker at Little Wakering was also summoned, and he arrived with coffin and hearse ready to take Elizabeth, her injured brother and, of course, the contraband overland. With her injured brother lying in the coffin, Elizabeth – deep in 'mourning' with her black shawl wrapped around her head – made her way to safety. Nothing would stop her now – not even when she had the unexpected misfortune of bumping into a customs officer close to Leigh Hill. According to the local legend, he simply tipped his hat and cast his eyes towards the ground in solemn respect, blissfully unaware of what was really passing before him.

Chapter Three

Murderers

Ever since Cain killed Abel, man has continued to take the life of another human being in order to get what he wants and there has been no shortage of people in Essex willing to carry out the ultimate crime.

Men and women from all walks of life – including royalty – have turned to murder within the county's boundaries. The motive for these acts of atrocity can vary greatly. Essex has seen it all: murder for political and religious reasons, even pride, and, of course, the route of all evil…the love of money.

Richard II

Richard II was not the only king of England to go to the grave with blood on his hands. There are many tales of skulduggery, treachery and, ultimately, murder within the royal court over the years. Many a ruler has ordered the death of someone who has stood in their way.

However, the abduction of the Duke of Gloucester from his Essex castle and subsequent murder in 1397, still sits high on the list of dastardly deeds carried out by monarchs. There are many theories surrounding the death of Thomas of Woodstock, Duke of Gloucester, the most colourful of which is perhaps the reason the incident has a lasting place in our history books. If that version is to be believed – even though murder is often carried out by cowards – few murders can have been so cowardly.

The Duke of Gloucester was the son of Edward III and uncle to Richard II. When the young Richard came to the throne in 1377, he was just ten years old. It meant people like the Duke held much influence over him. He was too young to make important decisions and relied on the advice of others. As a consequence, the Duke became very powerful and, along with some fellow noblemen, was ultimately responsible for running the country.

Of course, as the boy king got older, things began to change and the Duke lost some of his influence. The Duke was particularly keen to continue hostilities with France. The French had been a big problem during the early reign of Richard II. However, the young monarch, now a man able to make his own decisions, signed a truce with France and even married the French King's daughter. It was not a popular move and angered many Englishmen. In a bid to regain some influence, it is thought the Duke, hoping to take advantage of the discontent among the people, plotted against his nephew.

Little remains of Pleshey Castle where Richard II came to betray the Duke of Gloucester.

The village sign at Pleshey suggests just how important the castle once was.

Richard was fully aware of the Duke's intentions and decided to strike the first blow. There was nothing spontaneous about the murder of the Duke of Gloucester. It was pre-meditated and came during the period of Richard's reign known as 'the tyranny' – in which the King took revenge on his enemies and those who had manipulated him throughout his younger years.

There is little doubt the Duke was no saint. He was ambitious and unscrupulous, and the King had good reason to suspect him of conspiracy. Richard had also earlier watched the Duke and his fellow noblemen order the executions of some of his own friends who were becoming too powerful for their liking. Perhaps the monarch could not be blamed for seeking revenge. However, if the most famous version of the death of the Duke of Gloucester is to be believed, he was not simply arrested and charged, but kidnapped. There was certainly to be no trial.

The Duke thought Richard had arrived at his stronghold in Pleshey, north of Chelmsford, on a social visit, or so the story goes. Pleshey Castle was an impressive household of royal grandeur, quite fitting for one of the most powerful noblemen in England. The Duke and his family were used to entertaining and would have, no doubt, warmly greeted the monarch on arrival. There was no hint of any mischief or foul play as the party sat down for dinner. One can only imagine what was going through the King's head when he lay in his comfortable bed at Pleshey Castle that night, for the next day, having persuaded the Duke to travel with him to London to meet some people on pretence of business, the royal party set off – and the Duke of Gloucester did not return to his home alive. According to this particular version of the story, the Duke still had no idea of the fate that awaited him. In the evening, the party arrived at Stratford. It was late and dark when the King's men gradually, and quite deliberately, edged further ahead of the Duke's entourage, so that there was a wide gap between them. This was when the Duke and his servants were confronted by a band of armed men. The Duke was informed that he was under arrest, on the orders of the King. Quite stunned and believing it to be almost a joke, he replied that it was impossible, as at that very minute he was travelling with the King himself. He is reputed to have called to the King in the distance in a bid to get him to turn back. Of course, his cries fell on deaf ears. It is said the callous monarch never turned his head and continued his journey to London.

The Duke was put on a barge in the Thames and transferred to a ship that set sail for Calais – where he was imprisoned. It is not known how long he remained a captive before his ordeal ended. It is believed he was suffocated under a feather mattress in the bedroom of an inn. However the Duke met his fate – and the above version may be more fiction than fact, according to the majority of historians – there is little doubt the murder was carried out on the King's authority.

The story does not have a happy ending, but some may say it has a just one. Richard II received his comeuppance just a couple of years after the murder of his uncle. In fact, he suffered a similar fate. Richard was himself imprisoned – by his cousin who proclaimed himself King Henry IV. And, just like the Duke of Gloucester, some claim Richard was murdered on the orders of the new monarch. It would have perhaps been a fitting end for a man probably responsible for one of the most cowardly acts in the county of Essex. John Holand – half-brother of Richard II and a noted henchman of the King – also received his comeuppance. Holand, who some say may have been physically responsible for the reputed ambush of the Duke, was himself seized at Pleshey and executed, following a conspiracy against the new monarch.

The village of Pleshey still boasts evidence of the fine castle that once stood there, even if little of the brickwork remains. It is a charming and peaceful place, seemingly a world away from anything of importance. William Shakespeare famously spoke of it in his play *Richard II*.

Bloody Mary

Mary I was a queen who gained a reputation. It was not a good one, however.

Her reign is remembered for little else than her relentless persecution of Protestant 'heretics'. She was not the only monarch to use her power to 'murder' innocent people, but an incredible 300 or so opponents of Catholicism were cruelly executed during her reign in the 1550s. The nickname 'Bloody Mary' was totally justified. Even though Mary Tudor was a one-time Essex resident, the county did not get off lightly when she came to the throne. It is believed more than seventy of her victims hailed from within its boundaries – more than any other county in England.

Mary would have had much time at New Hall in which to plot her revenge.

Mary is still a much-maligned monarch and rightly so, but she herself led a life where death was always just around the corner. There can be little doubt her heart was hardened by her upbringing. Her father, King Henry VIII, was also not unaccustomed to condemning to death anyone who stood in his way. At least Catherine of Aragon, Mary's mother and the King's first wife, was spared execution, unlike some of his later wives, but mother and daughter were still treated abominably.

As Anne Boleyn, an Essex girl, came to prominence, poor Mary and her mother lived under the constant threat of death. Anne – who became the King's second wife – was intent on seeing the pair executed. Henry owned many palaces in Essex. The Princess Mary also resided at Copped Hall, near Epping, though it was at New Hall – her father's grand property at Boreham on the outskirts of Chelmsford – that she spent her most notable years of seclusion before becoming queen. The building, then called Beaulieu, is now home to a famous school. Henry sent Mary there during her enforced separation from her mother. She was still a teenager when her parents' marriage was declared void. Mary wrote letters to her father from New Hall, claiming that she still believed she was the legal heir to the throne. It must have been tough to watch from the sidelines, a virtual prisoner in her own home, as her father wedded his new love – a woman that Mary could not abide. Mary considered New Hall to be one of her favourite homes, but had a particular dislike of some of the rooms. She labelled the apartment Anne had slept with her father in as the 'infernal' chamber. You perhaps cannot blame her. And it must have felt like salt was rubbed in the wound when she was then forced to leave the house to make way for George Boleyn, the brother of Anne, for a period following the latter's marriage to the King.

Of course, it all turned sour for Anne Boleyn too and once she had been removed from the scene, Mary returned to New Hall. Henry's third wife – Jane Seymour – was much kinder to Mary. However, Mary's devout Catholicism always remained a problem. She was forced to observe her faith privately within the walls of her various homes, another being Hunsdon, near Harlow, just over the border in Hertfordshire. When her half-brother Edward VI became king following the death of Henry, Mary was next in line to the throne and

A boat was kept at Maldon in case Mary had to flee her enemies.

became a figurehead for Catholic rebels intent on seeing her become Queen of England. On the flip side, there were those that were willing to stop at nothing to ensure England remained a Protestant country, which meant Mary's life was also in danger, perhaps now more than ever. Her loyal followers would remove her from New Hall whenever they felt there was a real risk of assassination. Her hideaway was a property at Woodham Walter, just a couple of miles from Maldon. There she remained in the care of the Fitzwalters, a prominent and loyal Essex family. A boat was kept at Maldon — a town at the head of the Blackwater Estuary — if ever Mary needed to be smuggled abroad should things become too serious.

However, when Edward VI died and Lady Jane Grey was briefly ushered to the throne in a bid to ensure a Protestant succession, Mary was first moved to Hunsdon and then further into East Anglia. It was feared she may indeed have been in need of a boat to Europe, but the tide turned in her favour. She was declared the rightful heir to the throne, and Lady Jane Grey's reign lasted just nine days.

In July 1553, Mary was back at New Hall. A few days later, she made for London, stopping at Ingatestone Hall, home of Sir William Petre, and the royal palace at Havering-atte-Bower, the former home of her mother and another childhood residence. Finally, she met her half-sister Elizabeth at Wanstead, where they embraced. Also there to greet her were thousands of noblemen, knights and servants. The royal entourage then made its way to the capital and Mary Tudor was crowned Queen of England.

In the few years Mary reigned, she certainly left her mark. Her main aim on taking up the throne was to re-establish England as a Catholic country. And nothing would stop her in trying to achieve that. Her reign became one of terror, her persecution of extreme Protestants relentless.

Examples of her cruelty can be found throughout the county of Essex. Memorials to Protestants martyred during her reign are plentiful. 'Heretics' suffered the most appalling deaths, and not just by burning. The martyrdom of George 'Trudge-Over-the-World' Eagles, in the now county town of Chelmsford, is typical of the lengths Mary and her loyal subjects would go in an attempt to dissuade people from practising the Protestant faith. Eagles earned his nickname by 'trudging' from town to town preaching. Such was his reputation, a reward was offered for his capture. Eagles was eventually arrested and sentenced to be hanged, drawn and quartered. On leaving his prison cell in Chelmsford, he was tied to a sledge and dragged to the gallows. Eagles was hanged for a short time and then cut down before he was dead. The executioner then hacked at his neck with a blunt cleaver. His heart was torn out and his head, when finally severed, stuck on a pole and fixed to the market cross. The quartered body was displayed in four different parts of the county as a warning to all.

The reign of Mary I proved to be a turbulent one. Under her half-sister, Elizabeth I, England again became a Protestant country and, it has to be said, this time Catholics were cruelly put to death once more. However, it was never on the same scale as during the reign of Bloody Mary – a true villain of Essex.

Frances Howard

Poet and courtier Thomas Overbury was made to pay for aiming his pen in the direction of the Countess of Essex, *née* Frances Howard of Audley End, Saffron Walden.

His famous poem *A Wife*, which was circulated throughout the royal court of James I, was seen as an indirect attack on her

The Howard family vault is in the parish church at Saffron Walden.

character. But Frances was to gain her revenge in the deadliest fashion. She had him murdered in what was one of the most sensational crimes in British history.

Mystery still surrounds the death of Overbury, the victim in this infamous scandal at court, but it is generally accepted that Frances Howard, then the wife of Robert Devereux, 3rd Earl of Essex, was the brains behind the murder, which took place in 1613.

Overbury was poisoned while imprisoned in the Tower of London. He was all that stood in the way of a union between Frances and Robert Carr, who later became Earl of Somerset. Frances' marriage to Devereux had been a disaster. It had been arranged for political reasons and the two were teenagers at the time. While still married, Frances met and fell in love with Carr, the favourite of King James. Overbury was the personal adviser to Carr and even used his literary talent to good effect, penning his friend's love letters. However, when things started to get serious, Overbury became nervous and did all he could to end the match. An annulment of the marriage of Frances and Devereux had been sought, and Overbury feared the prospective union of Frances and Carr would reduce the influence he held over Carr, and ultimately the King. Overbury was the brains behind the inarticulate Carr and, because of Carr's close relationship with James, became a sort of unofficial secretary to the presiding monarch. The poet held much influence at court and the last thing he wanted, for political reasons, was an alliance with the Howards.

Frances and Carr now found Overbury standing in the way of their planned union. There was no doubt Overbury was a troublemaker at court and the King also wanted to see the back of him. He offered him a post abroad, but the writer refused to go. The King was furious and had him imprisoned in the Tower for contempt. However, it was just an excuse to get him out of the way while Frances' marriage could be annulled and her subsequent union with Carr arranged.

Overbury died in prison less than two weeks before the marriage of Frances and Devereux was officially ended. A few months later, Frances wed Carr.

Everything appeared to be rosy for the new couple and the King bestowed further honours upon his favourite. However, some two years after the death of Overbury, it all went wrong for them. People had assumed that Overbury, who was in prison for more than four months, had died of natural causes, but, in 1615, Sir Gervase Elwes, Lieutenant of the Tower, admitted that he had known about a plot to kill the prisoner. In his confession, he implicated others, including Frances and Carr.

During subsequent trials, Frances became one of the most hated figures in the country. The public were in no doubt she was the one behind the murder. She was depicted as a whore and a witch for first seducing Carr, the King's most cherished, and then using magic potions to poison Overbury.

Frances certainly had a motive for seeing off Overbury. It is little wonder she took offence to his famous poem, *A Wife*. The work highlighted the virtues a woman needed to possess if she was to become a suitable spouse. It was suggested to Frances that the aim of the poem was to open the eyes of Carr, with the result that he would discover the true character of the woman he was about to marry. Overbury also penned letters to Carr from his prison cell that claimed he would disclose the whole truth about his master and the woman he was about to wed. That was a good enough reason for Carr and Frances to silence Overbury forever, and some claim Frances had even tried to have the poet murdered before he was imprisoned.

However, once behind bars, Frances decided to complete the job, though she did not need magic potions. She employed a small team of dependants to carry out the dirty work. They obtained the poison and introduced it into the food sent to the prisoner.

Elwes and three others were executed for their part in the plot. As for Frances, she pleaded guilty to the murder of Overbury, but her life was spared. The King claimed her confession and penitence was good reason to let her live. However, both she and her husband were imprisoned themselves in the Tower and spent many years behind bars, before being released and spending the rest of their lives in obscurity.

Frances died in 1632. She was buried at Saffron Walden, home of the family seat. Her father was Thomas Howard, 1st Earl of Suffolk – builder of the impressive mansion at Audley End, one of Britain's grandest houses.

'Captain' Dougal

'Captain' Dougal – despite the title – was no military hero. Samuel Herbert Dougal, to give this villain of Essex his full name, was also a forger, though it was murder for which he gained lasting notoriety.

Newspapers described his trial as one of the most sensational of modern times. It was, perhaps, because 'Captain' Dougal almost got away with the murder of his partner, despite the audacity of the crime. The body of Camille Holland was not discovered until some four years after he killed her at their remote farm near Clavering, just south-west of Saffron Walden, in 1899.

The couple had not been together long. Dougal, posing as a successful ex-army officer, was a charmer and swept the spinster off her feet. Both were in their fifties at the time and are believed to have met via a newspaper advert. Camille was blissfully unaware of Dougal's past. He had been married three times and his third wife was still alive when he persuaded Camille to move into the isolated Coldhams Farm with him, a property that they obtained via her money and renamed Moat Farm. She also did not know that Dougal had previously been sentenced to 12 months of hard labour for forgery.

Dougal did serve the Royal Engineers for many years, but it was as a humble clerk and it is thought he never ever attained a commissioned rank. However, he took full advantage of the uniform and developed quite a reputation for the ladies. It appears

Dougal only had one thing on his mind when he started to court the wealthy Camille – getting his hands on her fortune.

Some three weeks after moving to the farm, Camille vanished. Dougal told the servant his mistress had gone to London. The reality was that Dougal had shot Camille dead. He hid the corpse in a drainage ditch at the farm, which he later had filled in, and it remained there until 1903.

When Camille did not 'return' from the capital, Dougal informed the servant that she had gone on holiday and would not be coming back for some time. This was too much for his employee. She herself had been the attention of some unwanted advances from her boss and was petrified at the thought of staying in the house alone with him. She packed her bags and left.

Dougal kept up the pretence, telling people that Camille was staying with friends, but it was not long before another woman was living with the 'captain' at the farm. It was his third and legal wife, though the neighbours were told it was his widowed daughter. Eventually the real Mrs Dougal discovered he was getting up to more mischief with servants and also left.

Meanwhile, Dougal had set about getting his hands on Camille's money, forging cheques and letters to the bank. Nobody at the bank was suspicious and even Camille's family, it appears, went along with the idea that she was living elsewhere with friends. However, Dougal must have surely realised that he could not keep up the act forever. In the end, local gossip prompted the police to make some enquiries, as it was so long since anyone had seen Camille. Some neighbours even believed that she might have been a prisoner in her own house.

Eventually Dougal was arrested and charged with forgery. It gave the police an excuse to search the farm, and the body of Camille Holland was found. Dougal was hanged for murder that same year and poor Camille was finally laid to rest. However, for a long time, superstitious neighbours were reluctant to pass the farm because of the evil that had occurred there. Some even reported they could still hear Camille playing her beloved piano.

Chapter Four

Rebels

A rebel with a cause may not always be a villain. Some have changed the course of history for the better due to their actions. It is a noble act to stand up and fight for the benefit of others. However, many rebellions in Essex have come at a huge cost. Innocent lives have been lost and the motives of the rebels have not always been altruistic.

John Ball

The infamous Peasants' Revolt of 1381 started and finished in Essex. Colchester priest, John Ball, was one of the leaders, and certainly the voice of the rebellion against social injustice. To some, such as writer William Morris, who penned the famous *A Dream of John Ball*, this passionate clergyman was a hero, but the revolt was not pretty and many lost their lives. Ball himself paid the ultimate price.

Ball believed that all men were born equal. He called on the people to overthrow the Government and set up a commonwealth based on social equality. In the long-suffering peasants of Essex and Kent, he found a captive audience. There was much unrest in the second half of the fourteenth century. The Black Death had wiped out about a third of the population and there was a shortage

John Ball called on the peasants to rebel.

of agricultural labourers, which drove up wages and encouraged landlords to claim their full dues from their tenant villeins.

It was, however, the introduction of a new poll tax that really sparked the flame of rebellion. The war with France had proved costly and the King needed to boost the coffers. The already simmering villeins saw it as the last straw. It led to riots throughout the country – though the revolt was focused on Essex and Kent, starting in the former county.

It was at Brentwood where things started to turn really ugly. A tax commissioner was sent to investigate the non-payment of taxes and to carry out a new tax census. However, he and his men were lucky to escape with their lives. Fishermen and labourers from the Thames-side communities of Fobbing, Corringham and Stanford-le-Hope, were in Brentwood to greet him and they had no intention of dipping into their pockets. He was savagely attacked. Undeterred, the Chief Justice arrived a few days later to sort out the matter. Once again, he was met by an angry mob made up of men from various parishes. A number of officers were killed. Riots ensued, with the peasants marching on villages and towns to recruit more members. The mob grew larger as thousands joined the rebellion – some reluctantly. Villagers often had little choice. If they did not join the revolt, they could have had their own homes ransacked or even lost their lives. Unpopular lords were murdered and estate records, with proof of the services the villeins owed their lords, destroyed. The home of the Sheriff of Essex, in Coggeshall, was one of the properties plundered.

There was a similar uprising in Kent, led by Wat Tyler. It was the Kent insurgents, joined by some of the agitators from Essex, who

The Peasants' Revolt of 1381 was said to have started close to the now ruined chapel in Brentwood high street.

famously stormed the gaol at Maidstone and freed Ball. He had been jailed – not for the first time – for upsetting the Archbishop of Canterbury with his strong political and religious views. It was shortly after his release that he preached his famous sermon at Blackheath, calling on the people to overthrow the Government. It was inevitable that the Essex and Kent movements should unite and head for London, where more riots ensued, the burning and ravaging showing no sign of halting.

King Richard II had to act and decided to meet the rebels at Mile End. Faced with a vast armed mob, it was perhaps not surprising he agreed to meet their demands. Believing the monarch would fulfil his promise to abolish villeinage and pardon the rebels, the crowd dispersed. But the promise proved to be a hollow one, and he was forced to confront the rebels again at Smithfield. This time Tyler, the leader of the movement, was stabbed and killed. The young Richard may have been seen as the real villain for breaking his word, but you could not fail to admire his bravery in risking his own life to confront the rebels. He was just fourteen at the time. Still believing the King would meet their demands, the agitators – left reeling by the death of Tyler – dispersed again, though the King later rode into Chelmsford and officially revoked all the previous pledges he had made.

The dwindling rebels were hunted down by the King's forces and one group fled to Billericay, reputedly to Norsey Wood on the outskirts of the town. Richard's powerful army, led by the Earl of Buckingham, proved too strong for the peasants, most only armed with shovels and forks, the tools of their trade. It is thought about 500 rebels were massacred. The lucky ones managed to flee to safety. Though there were pockets of resistance, the Norsey Wood incident is generally regarded as the end of the uprising.

The leaders of the movement who were still alive were rounded up and executed, Ball being one of them. He was hanged, drawn and quartered as a traitor under the watchful eye of the King.

It is said about 100,000 peasants from Essex and Kent were involved in the march to London. John Ball was undoubtedly the inspiration for many of those. His intentions may have been admirable in trying to bring justice to the common man, but this controversial priest of St James the Great Church, Colchester, was not willing to achieve that aim through peaceful means. He wanted it at whatever the cost. And, in terms of blood shed, that cost was to be extremely high.

Charles Lucas

It is not often a memorial is erected in honour of a bad guy. Those seeking any visible tribute to the likes of Dick Turpin or Matthew Hopkins in the vicinity of their crimes, as famous as those two are, will have little joy. Truthfully, Sir Charles Lucas does not actually fit in the same category as those two rogues, but he was certainly a bad man in the eyes of Colchester folk during the Civil War. A brave soldier he may have been, but he was partly responsible for many deaths and much hardship, not to mention almost the entire destruction of the town.

Lucas received his comeuppance following the Siege of Colchester – one of the most famous incidents in the town's history, and a pivotal event in the Civil War. The memorial, which

The memorial to Royalists Sir Charles Lucas and Sir George Lisle in the grounds of Colchester Castle.

marks the spot where he and fellow Royalist commander Sir George Lisle were executed by Parliamentarian forces, stands outside Colchester Castle.

Essex and Colchester remained almost untouched by the Civil War. Unlike other counties, residents were generally spared its horrors until it was virtually all over. The Siege of Colchester in 1648 certainly made up for the lack of prior action, however.

The event took place in what many describe as the Second Civil War. Charles I was already in prison and the Parliamentarians were in control, but the Royalists fought back, with several uprisings in various locations throughout the country. However, there was little public support for them. The people had endured enough and by now just longed for peace.

Lucas had taken control of the Royalist Army in Essex, which had grown to a considerable size. He was a devout Royalist and a Colchester resident. The family home was at St John's Green, so it was quite probable that he marched to Colchester in the hope his home town would welcome him and his troops. However, Colchester, on the whole, supported Parliament during the Civil War, and residents wanted to see the back of Lucas, their mistrust of him arising early on in the conflict because of his family's staunch loyalty to the monarch.

The people of Colchester did not have the means to send Lucas and his arriving army packing, but there was someone who did. Sir Thomas Fairfax was the man in command of the Parliamentarian Army. He had been on the tail of Lucas' troops and the first skirmish

Old Siege House in Colchester.

actually took place on the outskirts of the town. The Royalists retreated inside the town walls, which proved to be their downfall. They were surrounded. Fairfax established his headquarters at Lexden and waited. He decided he would starve them out.

The Royalists must have known their days were numbered. At first they managed to get supplies from ships docked at The Hythe, Colchester's port, but Fairfax soon cut off their route to the river. Unless outside help arrived, the Royalists were doomed. They must have feared nobody would come to their aid, however. There had been other Royalist uprisings, but elsewhere in the country. They were on their own and Fairfax knew it. The Royalists had to resort to sorties after dark in order to get fresh supplies for themselves and the people of the town who were also 'imprisoned' within the town walls. Fairfax was himself criticised for not letting the residents out. When supplies were dwindling, many sent messages pleading to be 'freed'. Some did try to leave the town and, it was claimed, were even shot at by the Parliamentarians who had come to rescue them. Fairfax later defended what looked like a heartless act by claiming that the more people left in the town, the less there would be to eat, which meant the siege would end sooner rather

Even today the Old Siege House houses evidence of violent duels in days-gone-by, with the clearly visible bullet holes on the side of the building.

than later. He argued it was purely a military decision not to 'free' the residents cooped up in their own town with the 'enemy'. Once the food had gone, the Royalists would have to surrender. This was indeed the case, but they left it late. The people were starving and resorted to eating rats once the cats and dogs had been consumed.

Lucas may have been misguided in his actions, but one cannot fault his bravery. He was also one of the top cavalry officers of the day, a brilliant commander. He himself is believed to have personally led one attempt to break free. It took place in the area of East Bridge. The Royalists inflicted casualties, but ultimately had to retreat. The Old Siege House, complete with bullet holes obtained during that particular skirmish, still stands in the town as another reminder of this incredible conflict between Parliament and the monarchy.

After eleven weeks, Lucas finally surrendered. His Royalist troops had their lives spared, but Lucas and fellow commander Sir George Lisle were executed. Both bravely faced the firing squad, Lisle even cracking a joke. He is reputed to have told his executioners to move closer. One replied they were close enough, to which Lisle quipped, 'I have been nearer when you have missed me.'

To the Royalists, Lucas and Lisle were heroes. At the Restoration, when Charles II came to the throne, a memorial was erected at the castle that claimed their deaths were nothing short of murder. However, to the people of Colchester in 1648, Lucas and Lisle were far from heroes. The three-month siege left many scars. Houses were wrecked and some areas of the town were virtually devastated, many prominent buildings falling. The famous St Botolph's Priory may have 'survived' Henry VIII's Dissolution of the Monasteries, but not the war games of Fairfax and Lucas.

The ordinary people of Colchester, through no fault of their own, had found themselves trapped within their own town walls, and were made to pay a huge price. There were reports of women being raped and men murdered from within the walls during those never-ending eleven weeks. Many lost their lives, while the lucky ones emerged half-starving and probably homeless. The Parliamentarians only rubbed salt into the wound, however. They promised to spare the town from plunder so long as the residents paid a fine for 'sheltering' the King's soldiers! The fine was a significant one too – another blow to people who had lost much because of a Royalist cause they had themselves opposed.

St Botolph's Priory felt the full force of hostilities during the Siege of Colchester.

Diarist John Evelyn remarked on how Colchester had been demolished by the siege, though it did recover – if not for long. Sadly, for those embattled residents worse was to follow, something even deadlier than the English Civil War. In 1665-6, the Great Plague came to town and wiped out about half of the population of Colchester.

Geoffrey de Mandeville, 1st Earl of Essex

Geoffrey de Mandeville, 1st Earl of Essex, did not exactly do the county proud. He manipulated his way to power and ended up being responsible for the massacre of many innocent people when he led a bloody rebellion against King Stephen, the man who created his earldom. He was arguably the cruellest of the lawless barons that held much sway at the time. Even though de Mandeville did much for the town of Saffron Walden, known simply as Walden in the twelfth century, it is all perhaps overshadowed by his atrocities on the battlefield.

It was the grandfather of Geoffrey de Mandeville – who also shared the same Christian name – that was granted the manor of Walden, as well as other lands throughout Essex. This was in recognition of his services to William the Conqueror. However, when the younger Geoffrey de Mandeville came into his inheritance, he had to recover lost lands and offices, his father having died owing a debt to the Crown. One of those offices was the post of Constable of the Tower of London, which both his father and grandfather had held.

Little remains of Saffron Walden Castle – former home of Geoffrey de Mandeville.

Playing a deadly game with two people that longed for the throne of England initially helped de Mandeville achieve his aims and much more besides.

The death of Henry I in 1135 plunged England into civil war. The successor to the throne was not obvious. Both Stephen, the King's nephew, and Matilda (also known as Maud), the King's daughter and rightful heir, claimed it for their own. Because both claimants to the throne needed support from the barons, de Mandeville found himself in a strong position and he used his power to good effect. He was to change allegiance on more than one occasion, seemingly choosing the side that was best for him.

De Mandeville first supported Stephen and was rewarded with the earldom of Essex in 1140. It is believed to have been the earliest charter granting an English earldom. However, it was not long before he switched sides, when Matilda, eager to gain his support, lured him over with – among other things – a charter permitting him to move the market at nearby Newport into his castle at Walden. This was important in order to stimulate growth and ensure the future success of the town. Saffron Walden has been a market town ever since.

The prosperity of Saffron Walden has much to do with Geoffrey de Mandeville, who was willing to betray a king in order for it to become a market town.

Soon de Mandeville was back with Stephen, after the offer of more 'bribes'. But, when de Mandeville again conspired with Matilda in 1142, his dangerous game had gone too far. Stephen, after seeing off Matilda, discovered de Mandeville's final betrayal and he was arrested. The new monarch offered de Mandeville a choice. He could forfeit his land, including his castles at Walden and Pleshey (the latter was built by his grandfather), or be executed. Perhaps, unsurprisingly, he chose the former option. However, it has been recorded that he departed the royal court 'like a vicious and rider-less horse, kicking and biting'.

De Mandeville was certainly not content to slip into the shadows and he began to plot a terrible revenge. He gathered a large army and led a rebellion against Stephen. He concentrated on the Fens. However, he did not lead like he was in charge of an army, but as though he was the chief of a gang of outlaws and thugs. All kinds of savage acts were committed. Abbeys and villages were ransacked and the local people were left traumatised by his ruthless massacring. Cambridge, which was loyal to Stephen, was among his targets – many people were put to death and the city was set on fire. The terrible reign of de Mandeville ended at Burwell in 1144, when an arrow fatally wounded him.

De Mandeville did much for Walden. As well as establishing it as a market town, he founded the priory that became an abbey and probably built the castle. However, because of his outrages against the Church in the Fens, he was excommunicated following his death and denied burial in the priory he had himself established.

Robert Fitzwalter

Robert Fitzwalter was not a loyal servant of King John, and used his position of power in an attempt to overthrow the unpopular monarch. As leader of the rebel barons, he was actively involved in forcing John to seal the famous *Magna Carta* in 1215, and then ensuring the King honoured its terms. When John failed to keep his side of the bargain, Fitzwalter – under the proud title of 'Marshal of the Army of God and Holy Church' – was instrumental in seeing off the King for good.

Priory Church at Little Dunmow, the resting place of Robert Fitzwalter.

Many may be surprised to see Fitzwalter in a book about the villains of Essex. The Lord of Dunmow is a hero to most. Indeed, the *Magna Carta* – sealed at Runnymede – is arguably the most important document in English constitutional history. One of its main aims was to ensure the monarch was not above the law. It meant the ordinary man was granted greater freedom and justice. One of the sixty-plus clauses states that the law should be fair to all, and that no man will be punished without going through a proper legal system.

However, the twenty-five barons commissioned to ensure that the terms were met did not have just the country at heart. Needless to say, there were personal motives too. John had abused feudal rights and taxed the barons heavily. In truth, the *Magna Carta* is largely concerned with barons' rights, more than those of the ordinary man. The barons had much power, but wanted more.

Many of the barons hailed from Essex, including Robert de Vere, Geoffrey de Mandeville (a later relation of the rebel who took up arms against King Stephen), Richard de Montfichet and William de Lanvallei. They were all prominent Essex men and put the county at the forefront of the rebellion. They, like many others, were not happy with the way the country was being governed. They threatened to take up arms against John unless he agreed to their reforms set out in the *Magna Carta*.

The King did not really have a choice in accepting the terms. The barons were not to be messed with, as they held much influence and had already amassed plenty of support. Fitzwalter himself was one of the most powerful men in England at the time.

John claimed the charter was sealed under duress, which it was. He had no intention of agreeing to all of its terms. Not long after the big day at Runnymede, John assembled an army consisting of his loyal followers and mercenaries. The Pope also sided with the King and annulled the charter – believing it to be against the belief of the divine right of kings. Those who had 'forced' John to seal the *Magna Carta* were excommunicated and orders were made to seize their lands.

Many fine Essex properties were destroyed or severely damaged when John's army marched upon the rebels. Mountfitchet Castle, near Stansted, was demolished and the King attempted to raze the fortress at Colchester too. The castles at Pleshey and Hedingham were also captured, though the latter did survive virtually intact, and still remains so today. The sieges involving John's army were the only action Hedingham Castle – home of Robert de Vere – ever saw. Abbeys and churches were pillaged too.

By early 1216, the rebels were in dire need of help, and it came from across the Channel. Fitzwalter may have himself personally travelled to France, on behalf of the barons, to renew an offer to put Louis, son of the reigning French monarch, on the English throne. It was not the first time the barons had tried to lure the French to their aid in this way. With the arrival of the French, the tide was soon to turn in favour of the rebels. The King and his men were driven north after some bitter fighting, and John himself died at Newark.

Fitzwalter and the barons eventually made their peace with Henry III, and were returned to favour, regaining their estates. A new revised version of the *Magna Carta* was also issued. Fitzwalter went on to serve the new monarch. He was actively involved in political affairs, and took part in a number of crusades before

King John and his forces captured
Hedingham Castle.

his death and burial at Dunmow Priory in 1235. The church at Little Dunmow, where he was laid to rest, is all that remains of the priory now.

Historians are divided over the true character of Robert Fitzwalter. Even the French, who came to the barons' rescue, were suspicious of him. Many felt he could not be trusted, simply for the fact that he had already betrayed one master — King John. Some have even suggested he was a coward. In 1203, he was given the joint command of a Norman fortress in France, which was surrendered without a fight. Though John came to his defence, claiming the surrender was at his instruction, many believed the monarch was just trying to cover up an act of cowardice or possibly some collusion with the French.

However, Fitzwalter was implicated in a plot to overthrow the King as early as 1212. The conspiracy involved killing John or abandoning him during a proposed expedition. The monarch got wind of the plan and had to abandon the trip. Fitzwalter was forced to take flight and his lands were seized, though they were restored the following year. There was no doubt the animosity between the King and Fitzwalter had been growing.

Some say he had another reason to hate the monarch. While in exile in France, Fitzwalter indicated that he believed his daughter Matilda, known as the 'Fair Maid of Essex', had been poisoned by one of the King's men. He claimed John had made lustful advances towards her. Furious with her rejection, the monarch got his revenge by killing her. There is no evidence to substantiate this claim and Fitzwalter may have concocted the story as justification for his own opposition to John, and to get others on his side. It would have painted an even darker picture of an already much-maligned figure. Even Fitzwalter's title 'Marshal of the Army of God and Holy Church' feels like it was designed to exonerate the barons and their actions.

The story of Matilda strangely took off much later in the sixteenth and seventeenth centuries, when a number of poems and plays were written about the alleged murder. Matilda was also known as 'Maid Marian', sparking a legend that Robin Hood's sweetheart was actually buried at Dunmow Priory.

Historians have spent much time trying to come up with the reasons why Fitzwalter was so opposed to the King. Perhaps his motives in leading the rebel barons were indeed simply for the good of the country, and not for revenge or for his own personal gain. Certainly, John was a harsh ruler, one you did not argue with. He could be cruel and would stop at nothing to get his own way. It is alleged he arranged for his nephew, who had a claim to the throne, to be murdered, and his scheming – with regard to his brother Richard I – has, of course, become legendary. Conspiracy and rebellion might have been the only way the barons could get their message across.

The true character of Robert Fitzwalter will never be known. He will remain a champion of English liberty to some, but to others will be viewed as a selfish, violent, perhaps even cowardly, rebel – one that was willing to stop at nothing to get what he wanted.

Chapter Five

Fraudsters, Embezzlers and Cheats

'Nobody likes a cheat.'

Few can say they have never bent the rules on occasions, but some have gone to great lengths to ensure they got what they wanted. Politicians and others in high places perhaps have further to fall if found guilty of cheating the system, and a number of Essex men and women of good standing have paid the price for going too far in their pursuit of riches and power.

Even the biggest house in the county came at a cost – not just financially – but to the man who used all manner of deceit to ensure it was built.

Thomas Howard, 1st Earl of Suffolk

Admiral Thomas Howard, 1st Earl of Suffolk, was determined to build the grandest house in England. He succeeded, but his mansion at Audley End, near Saffron Walden – erected on land obtained by his grandfather – came at a cost.

Howard and his wife would stop at nothing in order to fulfil their dream, resorting to embezzlement, extortion and bribery. It landed them before the notorious Star Chamber and ten days in the Tower of London. It is also fair to say the Earl of Suffolk was never quite the same man again after the scandal.

Born the son of Thomas Howard, 4th Duke of Norfolk, the early career of this hero-turned-villain was only positive. Howard excelled in the navy and was knighted for his role in the defeat of the Spanish Armada. Various titles were bestowed upon him. Even Lord Alfred Tennyson later immortalised him in his poem *The Revenge*. When James I came to the English throne, Howard was still a popular hero and the country could not get enough of him. One of his other notable achievements was directing the search of the Palace of Westminster cellars, that led to the discovery of the Gunpowder Plot.

The King had created Howard's earldom in 1603, making it even more important for him to have a residence suitable for entertaining the royal court. The construction of what was going to be the largest private house in England started in the same year. It was not completed until about 1614, the year in which Howard was appointed Lord High Treasurer of England. Howard himself claimed the mansion cost, including furniture, a massive £200,000. One of its contemporaries – Hatfield House in Hertfordshire – had been built at a fraction of that cost. The King

The construction of impressive Audley End came at a price.

was himself probably of the opinion Howard had gone over the top. On a visit, he famously and sarcastically remarked that Audley End was too great a house for a king, but might do for a Lord High Treasurer!

However, Howard's extravagance had got him into severe financial difficulties. The upkeep of the vast property was also astronomical and rumours of corruption started to circulate. In 1618, Howard was relieved of his duties as Lord High Treasurer when the King was made aware of his misconduct in the Treasury. There were suspicions he had embezzled money received from the Dutch, among other misdemeanours. In the following year, both he and his wife were found guilty of various charges. Many believe it was she who was the real mischief and brains behind the operation. She was accused of harassing the Crown's creditors and extorting bribes from them before they could obtain payment. It is said she barred them access to her husband, in his role as Lord High Treasurer, unless they rewarded her personally. The prosecuting Sir Francis Bacon compared Howard's wife to an exchange woman, keeping shop while her 'apprentice' Sir John Bingley – the Auditor of the Exchequer – touted for custom outside.

The Howards were committed to the Tower, but released after ten days on the agreement that they would pay a fine of £30,000. However, Howard further riled the King when he blatantly attempted to avoid seizure of his property by placing his lands in the hands of trustees and removing all the furniture from his houses. James threatened another visit in front of the Star Chamber, but relented, and even the fine was eventually reduced to £7,000.

Howard spent the rest of his life quietly, out of the public spotlight he so craved. He never managed to clear his debts and died some six years later.

Visitors to Audley End these days might argue that the impressive mansion was worth a little embezzlement, extortion and bribery. It is still an incredible property – even at one-third of its original size!

Richard the Extortioner

Sir Richard de Southchurch, perhaps better remembered as Richard the Extortioner, has often been described as a Robin

Hood in reverse. While the legend of Sherwood Forest robbed from the rich to give to the poor, Southchurch robbed from the poor to give to the rich – notably himself among them. Even more disturbing than this was the manner in which he did so. Southchurch abused his position of power. He might not have been the Sheriff of Nottingham – but he *was* the Sheriff of Essex.

Southchurch, who lived in the thirteenth century, was the owner of much land, including the manor to which he gained his title (Southchurch is now part of Southend-on-Sea). Already with much wealth, his position gave him the opportunity to become even wealthier – an opportunity he took. His main role as sheriff of the county during the Second Barons' War, was to provide stores for the royal forces when they were in Essex. He requisitioned all sorts of supplies in the name of Henry III. Poor farmers were deprived of their valuable crops or cattle, for what they thought was at least for the good of the country, though it is believed much of it ended up at Southchurch's own home. Not only had he gained property under false pretences, it is said he also kept the money given to him by the Crown to compensate the peasants he had 'robbed'. It is reputed he would also put in a bill for other supplies that had cost him nothing – those supplies that did legitimately go towards helping the King in battle against the rebel supporters of Simon de Montfort.

One of Southchurch's most famous requisitions was of a number of cocks. His excuse was that he needed them to help burn down the capital which was at the time in the control of the rebels. He claimed the birds were to have fire tied to their feet!

Southchurch was also reputed to have arrested innocent men and demanded payment in return for their freedom. Fines for even the guilty were often over the top and sometimes Southchurch, it was suggested, would refuse a prisoner bail, even after accepting the surety.

When Edward I came to the throne in 1272, the game looked up for Southchurch. A long list of charges were laid before him, but it appears he got off lightly. In later life he did, however, spend a spell behind bars and forfeited a number of his manors. There is some evidence he also treated the poor a little better and made provisions for them in his will. It might have been a little form of recompense from a man that was, not surprisingly, once much despised in the county of Essex.

John Attwood

Nineteenth-century politician John Attwood did not leave to chance his bid to win the seat of Harwich in the general election. It was not a case of what he could do for constituents if elected, but what he could do for constituents to ensure he *was* elected! He used his considerable wealth and influence to bribe electors, but he eventually received his comeuppance and lost the seat he had paid such a high price for. One MP – it was recorded in *Hansard* – remarked, with regard to what went on at Harwich, that 'the grossest cases of bribery had been proved that ever came before Parliament'.

Attwood, who made his fortune in the iron industry, was a man of enterprise and promoter of the railway. He was determined to represent the town, in order to steer through a private act to aid his project for a railway line between Harwich and Manningtree. He admitted his election victory in 1841 cost him £10,000 in bribes. Following the 1847 election, a select committee was set up to investigate further charges of corruption. Attwood was found guilty of election bribery and this time was ousted from his seat.

Bribes came in various forms. It is said he paid dozens of electors various sums of money in return for their vote in 1841. One father and son were barge owners and they reputedly bought a couple of new vessels with the money they had received – and then cheekily named one of the barges *Attwood*.

Hylands House was once home to disgraced MP, John Attwood.

Attwood owned much property and tenants would benefit from reduced rents in return for their vote. It was said at least one tenant was evicted from his home for not keeping his side of the bargain and voting for his landlord. However, one MP hinted that the residents of Harwich were almost just as much to blame as Attwood. *Hansard* records 'that when Mr Attwood went to canvass the borough, the electors thought it a good time to draw him out and make him open his purse-strings'.

Perhaps Attwood and his supporters' most ingenious way of ensuring election victory, was to arrange for boats to give free rides to the voters of his opponents. The vessels would be 'accidentally' diverted out to sea and, with the wind and tide against them, were not able to make it back to the harbour until the polling station had closed!

It has to be remembered that the number of electors in the nineteenth century was far fewer than it is today. It meant bribery was an option for those standing for election. In the mid-nineteenth century, Harwich was described as being in 'a most wretched state of corruption', but was by no means the only borough afflicted by election bribery. The problem was widespread and had existed for a long time.

An even more famous former Harwich MP – the diarist Samuel Pepys – was virtually guaranteed his seat when he stood for election in 1679. The electorate consisted of just thirty-two people – and all those were the members of the council. Pepys was working for the Admiralty at the time and any government nominee was certain of being elected. There is little doubt Pepys made it to Parliament on the 'Admiralty ticket'.

It was not until 1832 that the Reform Act established the principal of gaining office by popular vote, rather than by the votes of a chosen few, though there was still much corruption.

Maldon MP, Quintin Dick, served the town for some seventeen years from 1830, but that is no surprise when you learn he is said to have spent more than any other MP of his time in bribing constituents. It is reputed he coughed up a staggering £30,000 in 'electoral expenses'.

Dick was a former owner of Layer Marney Tower, the tallest surviving Tudor gatehouse in England. He bought the property, which is situated near Tiptree, in the mid-1830s and held it until his death in 1858. However, he spent most of his time in London, where he is remembered more for his opulent dinner parties than his political achievements. He is just another example of how corrupt politics had become in the nineteenth century, and Dick was certainly not the only politician in Essex, or throughout the country, who used their wealth and influence to further political ambitions. Attwood is perhaps unlucky because he lost his seat at Parliament. Others, such as Dick, just got away with it.

As for Attwood, he is little remembered outside of Essex these days – and even within it. The county town of Chelmsford has particular reason to acknowledge him, however. He was perhaps the most famous former owner of Hylands House, the stately home on the outskirts of the town. Attwood bought the property in 1839 and went about creating a grand estate fit to house a man of rising political and social status. The house was enlarged in order to reflect his position in society. However, Attwood spent most of his fortune on his impressive abode, and increasing debts – his speculations on the stock exchange also failing him – eventually forced him to part with it. He never really recovered from his banishment from Parliament and died in France a pauper.

Richard Rigby

It may have been no coincidence that Benjamin Disraeli – for his 1844 novel *Coningsby* – used the name 'Rigby' when creating a self-serving political parasite.

In the previous century, there was a Rigby who became suspiciously rich in his lucrative role as Paymaster of the Forces – a position he held for more than a dozen years from 1768. Richard Rigby, of Mistley, near Manningtree, is said to have had more than half a million pounds of surplus public money in his personal possession. He apparently treated the Government purse as his own, and freely used it to partake in his favourite hobbies of gambling and throwing wild parties at Mistley Hall – the family home.

Rigby was a brash and argumentative man, who made many political enemies. He spent much of his money – or the public's – in

Mistley Towers, a visible reminder of Richard Rigby.

The Naze Tower at Walton-on-the-Naze once held a secret.

an attempt to establish Mistley as a port and spa resort, but the project ultimately failed on account of his mounting debts. Fragments of his ambitious plan remain, notably a fountain enhanced by a model swan that was to form the centrepiece of the spa. Mistley is famed for a colony of swans that gather there. The twin towers of a proposed new-look church, designed by architect Robert Adam, have also become a notable local landmark. They are now known as Mistley Towers.

Rigby also became mixed up in another scandal of the day. He owned a fashionable tearoom in the prominent Naze Tower at Walton-on-the-Naze. More than scones and jam were reputedly on offer, however. It became a secret rendezvous and hideaway for gentlemen of high repute who wished to partake in extra-marital activities. It has been said famous actress and singer Martha Ray, long-term mistress of the Earl of Sandwich, secretly met James Hackman at the tower. The affair ended in tragedy; the jealous and possessive Hackman – unable to have Martha to himself – shot her dead as she came out of a theatre at Covent Garden.

Chapter Six

Adulterers, Bigamists and Mistresses

'Love outside marriage was once not viewed in the same way as it is today.'

Few now bat an eyelid where affairs are concerned, but over the centuries that has not always been the case. Despite the threat of scandal and social exclusion, many have been tempted to taste forbidden fruit. And some – such as a very famous monarch – appeared to have little concern for the third person in the triangle. However, with regard to one of his six famous wives – an Essex girl – she too gave as good as she got.

Henry VIII

King Henry VIII – not content with six wives – had many mistresses too. And Essex was home to a number of them. The county, due to its closeness to the capital but far enough away from prying eyes, was also the perfect location to bring up the illegitimate children of a monarch. However, the village of Blackmore, near Ingatestone, can claim to be the birthplace of the only illegitimate child Henry ever acknowledged.

It was at the Priory of St Laurence that Elizabeth 'Bessie' Blount gave birth to a boy – Henry Fitzroy. Bessie blossomed in the royal court and it has been suggested she was already involved with Henry senior when she was just fourteen, though she did not actually become his mistress until a few years later. However, she was not his only mistress. As first wife, Catherine of Aragon, endured at least six unsuccessful pregnancies, Henry was having his wicked way with a number

Henry VIII had much influence in Essex and is commemorated today at a North Weald Bassett pub.

of women. His relationship with Bessie did not threaten the royal marriage, even though Bessie was in the service of the Queen. Catherine had already given birth to a girl, who became Mary I, and the King was convinced a boy would eventually follow. It did, but via Bessie. When Henry discovered she was pregnant, he employed Cardinal Wolsey to make all the necessary arrangements. Bessie was packed off to the priory at Blackmore.

The King was delighted the baby was a boy. After its birth in 1519, he spent almost the entire summer in Essex, doting over his new son. The main residence of the original priory – of which only the church now remains – was known as Jericho House. It is said that when the King left court for no apparent reason, those that inquired as to his whereabouts were told – no doubt accompanied by a wink – that he had 'gone to Jericho'!

However, Henry soon felt it was no longer necessary to conceal his young son and bestowed many titles upon him as he grew older. There was little doubt it was the King's child, the son he could not have legitimately. The name 'Fitzroy' means 'son of the king'. If the boy had lived to beyond the age of seventeen, he might have had a claim to the throne. Some have even suggested that he did not die of natural causes and that Anne Boleyn and her brother George had him murdered for this reason.

A crown on the village sign is evidence of a royal 'secret' at Blackmore.

As for Bessie, needless to say, like most of Henry's mistresses, she was soon tossed to one side; Mary Boleyn, sister of Anne, became the new love of his life. In fact, after giving birth in Blackmore, Bessie never returned to court.

Even today, Blackmore does not overtly advertise the fact that it might have, if circumstances had been different, provided a future king of England. The village sign offers one clue – the picture of a gold crown.

Henry VIII had many connections to Essex. The county was strongly Protestant and he had palaces within its borders. New Hall at Boreham, near Chelmsford, previously the home of Thomas Boleyn – father of Anne – was among his favourite residences. Mary and Anne Boleyn, of Rochford, were also two of his 'conquests'. Henry spent many happy days wooing Anne at New Hall. He later took her replacement – Jane Seymour – to Terling, near Witham, another royal residence, following their marriage in 1536. It was Jane who finally produced the King's long-awaited legitimate son – Edward. Darker days were also spent in Essex. It is believed Henry hunted in Epping Forest while awaiting the signal informing him that the execution of Anne Boleyn had taken place.

Henry VIII gained notoriety for his misogynist ways, using women for his amusement and self-gain. However, not all of his mistresses were exactly squeaky clean or innocent themselves…

Anne & Mary Boleyn

Essex girl Anne Boleyn was executed after being found guilty of adultery. It is generally considered that the Queen of England was innocent of the charges laid before her, which also included incest and conspiracy against the King. However, some harsher critics are of the opinion she – and fellow members of the Boleyn family – got their just deserts.

Not one, but two members of the family became the mistress of Henry VIII, with Anne eventually 'getting' her man and becoming queen. The family, whose home was at Rochford, were ambitious and their dreams looked to have

The scheming Anne Boleyn, as depicted at the Queen's Head in Maldon, was an Essex girl through and through.

come true. Sadly, Henry became restless with the girl he was once infatuated with. When Anne failed to produce the male heir he so longed for, he tired of her and, not for the first time, his mistress – now wife – was cast aside for another woman.

Sister Mary knew exactly what it was like to be wooed by Henry and then rejected. She was mistress of the King before his roving eye landed on her sibling. Anne, seemingly not bothered by the way Mary had been tossed to one side once the amorous Henry had become bored with her, took the place of her sister and eventually became the second wife of the King.

Mary must have been green with envy. Not only had the King decided she was no longer required, but he had the audacity to fall for her sister of all people. Of course, in the end, Mary was perhaps the lucky one, as Anne was beheaded at the Tower of London in 1536.

Henry may have treated Mary poorly, but, like Anne, she was no angel. In her teens, she served in the court of Francis I of France. Said to be much prettier than Anne, she caught the eye of many a courtier. According to Francis himself, she was the most immoral woman at his court and he later labelled her a whore.

He is said to have nicknamed Mary his 'English mare' in reference to the number of times he had 'ridden' her!

It was on her return to England that Mary and Anne were officially 'introduced' to the King. Mary at first made the greater impression and was to become his mistress, from about 1522, even though she was married, having wed William Carey in 1520. Perhaps as a form of recompense, Carey was always treated well by the monarch and received plenty of grants. A son was born to Mary and her husband, though some suggested Henry was the real father.

Mary soon fell from favour, and Anne became the new apple of the King's eye. He had decided he wanted rid of Catherine of Aragon, his first wife, and started the long battle to divorce her, which led to England's momentous break from Roman Catholicism.

At first, Anne – maybe on the advice of her sister – refused to become the King's mistress, but the Boleyns had much to gain by keeping Henry happy. Father Thomas ardently encouraged the match, knowing it was another great opportunity for further preferment and power. He had already been created Viscount of Rochford in 1525, thanks to daughter Mary's willingness to amuse the King.

Anne was clever and decided to play hard to get. She was not content to remain as the King's mistress. She knew the more she refused his advances, the more he would want her. It proved to be the case. Henry was besotted. However, it was not long before Anne started to grow impatient, as Henry struggled to annul his marriage with Catherine. One day she remarked to her scheming uncle, the Duke of Norfolk, that she was wasting her time and youth waiting for Henry.

While still married to Catherine of Aragon, Henry at last started to treat Anne as though she was his wife. She was soon allowed into his bed, and famously on one occasion travelled with him to France to meet Francis I, proudly wearing jewellery that had been confiscated from Catherine. The two lovers spent many happy days at New Hall, Boreham, near Chelmsford – one of Henry's Essex palaces.

By the early part of 1533, Anne was pregnant and Henry secretly took her as his wife. It was an act of bigamy, as his marriage to Catherine had still not been annulled. It was finally pronounced null and void by Thomas Cranmer, Archbishop of Canterbury, by the spring and Anne was only then officially crowned Queen of England.

However, her problems were only just beginning. Anne wanted nothing more than the execution of Catherine and her daughter Mary, as she still feared them coming between her and her new husband. There were still plots to return the Catholic Catherine to power. And things soured further when Anne gave birth, not to a boy, but to a girl who later became Queen Elizabeth. Henry was convinced throughout her pregnancy that she was carrying a boy.

Anne was unpopular at court and had many enemies. She was deemed arrogant and malicious. One of her former lovers, Henry Percy, Earl of Northumberland, now referred to her as a whore – just like her sister Mary had been labelled in the royal court of France.

Henry also began to tire of his latest wife, and her overbearingly hot temper. It was not long before a woman of contrast, Jane Seymour, caught his eye. Anne demanded that the quiet and charming Jane be removed from court, but, of course, she was eventually to become the King's third wife.

Not even the death of Catherine of Aragon could save Anne now. When the latter gave birth to a stillborn son, it was the last straw for Henry. She, like Catherine, had also failed to provide him with a male heir to the throne.

It is more than probable Henry himself asked Thomas Cromwell, who was later created Earl of Essex, to come up with some incriminating evidence against Anne in order to justify a separation. He did just that, accusing her of adultery with five courtiers and also plotting the death of the King. One of the five courtiers was George Boleyn, her own brother and now Lord Rochford, and also a notorious womaniser. There was no doubt it was a trumped-up-charge, though some historians feel there may have been some truth in it. Certainly, Henry, in the latter days of their marriage, was becoming suspicious of Anne's behaviour and he may have had reason to.

The Duke of Norfolk, as Lord High Steward, presided over the trial, while another member of the family provided the damning evidence. Lady Jane Rochford, wife of George, testified that Anne had told her the King was impotent and was himself to blame for not producing a male heir. It 'explained'

Rochford Hall was home to the Boleyns.

why Anne might have gone in search of other men. If she could not have a child by the King, she might look elsewhere in becoming pregnant, and then attempt to pass the baby off as Henry's son and heir to the throne.

The Duke of Norfolk had the responsibility of sentencing his niece to death. Brother George was also executed.

As for sister Mary, she had already been banished from court – by Anne – following her secret marriage to William Stafford in 1534 – her first husband having died in 1528. The Boleyns were furious with the match, Stafford – who was of a low social position – not considered good enough for a family who believed status was everything. It must have been galling for poor Mary to have to watch Anne rise to power – knowing it could have been her – while brother George and father Thomas were bestowed with many privileges and titles. She even had to appeal to Cromwell for assistance and for some hope that she might one day regain favour at court. Mary never did, but at least she went on to enjoy a few years of retirement. Following the fall of her close family members, Mary inherited Rochford Hall and died there in 1543.

Incredibly, apart from Rochford Hall, which now houses a golf club, there are few reminders of the Boleyn family in the town itself. There is no statue or memorial to a former queen of England. Some might suggest it is because Anne Boleyn – perhaps the most scandalous woman to ever sit on the throne of England – and her manipulative family did not exactly do the county proud when they had their day in the limelight.

Kitty Canham

It must have been quite a sight to see the two husbands of Catherine 'Kitty' Canham walking arm in arm as her body was laid to rest in the village of Thorpe-le-Soken, north of Clacton-on-Sea. The men, both betrayed by this beautiful bigamist, were united in their grief at her funeral – their rivalry and differences put aside for her sake.

The tale of Kitty became headline news in 1752, the year of her lavish funeral in the parish church. She must have been quite a woman. Despite her unfaithfulness and lies, both of her husbands shed tears for her and went to great lengths to ensure she got the send-off they thought she still deserved.

Kitty was born in 1720, the daughter of a prosperous farmer at Beaumont Hall. She was a lively and popular child, the shining light of Thorpe-le-Soken. She had many suitors and presumably could pick and choose whom she liked.

For whatever reason, Kitty did turn down the advances of many, to such an extent that her parents became worried she would be left on the shelf. They reputedly warned her that she should not turn down the next man who offered his hand in marriage. That happened to be the vicar of Thorpe-le-Soken, Revd Alexander Gough. It is not known whether Kitty really did love Gough, or whether she was just trying to appease her parents, but the two were married in the mid-1740s. It appears Kitty was not suited to life as a vicar's wife. Tea parties and the like did not interest her and some have suggested Gough, like many men of the cloth, was a scholar more interested in his books than his wife. They were probably opposites and, though they may have been attracted in the first instance, their marriage was perhaps doomed from the start. Kitty craved a life of excitement and went in search of it. Without any notice, she disappeared one day and Gough was never to see her alive again.

Kitty headed for the bright lights of London and there enjoyed the high life. Men of importance were just as attracted to Kitty as the folk of Thorpe-le-Soken had been and it was not long before one of them offered his hand in marriage. Despite already having a husband, Kitty could not refuse the dashing Lord Dalmeny, son of the 2nd Earl of Rosebery. She accepted his proposal and her secret past life at the vicarage remained just that. Dalmeny was oblivious to her deception and the couple enjoyed a prolonged honeymoon touring Europe. It must have been three or four years of joy for Kitty and Dalmeny, while poor Gough had to endure the probably endless local gossip, still unaware of what had happened to his wife.

However, joy soon turned to despair for Dalmeny too. Kitty had not been in good health and fell ill in Verona. Knowing she was dying, she finally decided she had to reveal the truth and seek forgiveness. She wrote on a piece of paper that she wished to be buried at Thorpe-le-Soken, where her first husband still resided.

Dalmeny must have been stunned, but he still found it in his heart to forgive her. In those days, transferring a corpse across sea was not the done thing. The dead were usually buried in the country where they died. However, Dalmeny was determined to carry out the final wish of his beloved Kitty. Under an assumed name, posing as a merchant, he chartered a ship for England. Kitty's embalmed body was placed in a coffin that was then enclosed and sealed in a large wooden chest.

The vessel was bound for Harwich, but a storm blew it off course and it was forced into the mouth of the Colne. Smuggling was rife at the time and customs officers eyed it with suspicion. They boarded the vessel at The Hythe, Colchester, and, on seeing the wooden chest, became convinced it contained contraband. Dalmeny had to stop one of the officers from plunging his cutlass into the chest, drawing his own sword in the process. Now he had to reveal the truth: that the body of his 'wife' was inside. However, the officers were still not convinced and opened the coffin. Even when being confronted with a corpse, they were still not satisfied, now starting to believe the man before them was a murderer or guilty of some other foul play. He at last admitted that he was, in fact, a man of quality, the son of an earl. Dalmeny was still taken away for questioning and Kitty's body stored in the vestry at a nearby church. Meanwhile, Gough was summoned to identify the body and the two husbands of Kitty Canham came face to face for the first time. Gough admitted he at first wanted to kill Dalmeny, but could see that he too had also been duped and the two men united in sorrow.

Kitty Canham was laid to rest with great ceremony and, even today, her story lives on in Thorpe-le-Soken. Reputedly, the brother of Gough had warned the clergyman about Kitty. He predicted 'such a beautiful creature would play you a trick'. It seems Kitty did indeed play the ultimate trick – on two unsuspecting, but forgiving men.

Emma Hamilton

While Lord Horatio Nelson died a hero, mistress Lady Emma Hamilton died a villain in the eyes of the public. Both were shunned by polite society after Nelson – following years of courtship with the real love of his life – left his wife to move in with Emma and her husband Sir William. However, the famous naval commander found redemption in the hearts of the nation due to his exploits at sea, notably at the Battle of Trafalgar. That historic victory cost him his life, but ensured he went down in history as one of Britain's greatest sons.

Lord Nelson and the two women in his life, including Lady Hamilton, still adorn the wall of the former Three Cups hotel in Harwich.

There was no such grand finale for poor Emma, who died in exile virtually penniless. Lady Hamilton has always been viewed as the villain in one of the most famous love affairs of all time, though Nelson was himself no saint. It is just that his misdemeanours have generally faded into the shadows, the public preferring to concentrate on his momentous triumphs and heroic death at sea. And, it has to be said, there was no doubt his behaviour was at its worst when in the company of Emma.

Wild and fun-loving in her youth, and mistress to many, Emma was just as extravagant following the death of her husband and Nelson. She squandered the money left by the two men in her life and was imprisoned for debt before her death in France.

Nelson and Emma were not Essex residents, but they were regular visitors to the county, particularly its coast. A number of places, notably inns, claim to have been used as a secret rendezvous location by the lovers. Harwich was – as a seaport – a frequent haunt, the former Three Cups being the couple's most famous hideaway.

However, it is Southend-on-Sea that Emma was more than partial to. She was a regular visitor to the Royal Terrace, the best street in town. Southend was a fashionable resort at the beginning of the nineteenth century, and many figures of status could have been seen strolling up and down the promenade.

Both Nelson and Emma were married to others when they embarked on their love affair. They had at least one illegitimate child that survived to adulthood. Horatia was born in 1801 and given the surname 'Thompson'. Society believed Nelson and Emma were just the child's godparents who later 'adopted' her as an orphan.

Another secret child followed in late 1803 or early 1804, the year before Nelson's death. Some are of the opinion that it was born in the Southend area. It is said when the time came for Emma to give birth she was taken to a secret location; a little inland at Southchurch. It was suggested the property she was moved to belonged to Nelson's second lieutenant, James Woodward, who had presumably offered his childhood home in the hope it would be free from prying eyes. His sister – Mary Joscelyne – just happened to be a midwife and it was said she was called upon to help out in what became a difficult birth. The

Lady Hamilton stayed at grand Royal Terrace in Southend-on-Sea.

child was a girl and supposedly named Emma, but it is thought the baby did not survive more than a few weeks at most. It is quite probable Nelson was himself present at the birth.

There is no real evidence to back up the story. However, because of Essex's proximity to London, the couple's connections with Harwich and Emma's love of Southend, in particular, it might have more than a claim to be fact than the other numerous tales of illegitimate children born to perhaps the country's most famous adulterers.

Chapter Seven

Conspirators and Traitors

Betrayal is often viewed as the lowest point even a criminal can stoop to. And sometimes when the game is up, the more honourable miscreant has stubbornly refused to break the unwritten code of conduct and implicate another. However, some have not been so noble. Many have profited from exposing the misdemeanours of their fellow man, while others have switched allegiance for their own personal gain.

High treason was considered even worse than murder in days gone by. The punishment was more severe, with the treacherous offender to crown and country not just executed, but hanged, drawn and quartered. Despite the possibility of this awful fate, there was no shortage of people in Essex who believed the potential gain outweighed the risk.

Eadric Streona

One of the most significant acts of betrayal in English history occurred on an Essex battlefield in the eleventh century. It is claimed the Anglo-Saxons, under the command of Edmund Ironside, were defeated by the Danish Vikings because of the actions of one man – Eadric Streona.

The Vikings triumphed at Ashingdon thanks to a cruel act of betrayal.

The Battle of Ashingdon, in 1016, was the last time the Anglo-Saxon forces of Edmund – the King of England – met the Danish army of Canute in combat. Edmund had already defeated the invaders elsewhere and was expected to triumph once more to see off the Danes for good. Eadric of Mercia was one of the King's key commanders. However, he was not a loyal one and – when it came to the crunch – switched his allegiance at an enormous cost to the Anglo-Saxons. He is said to have led his men away from the battle at a crucial point, allowing the Danes to secure an unlikely victory.

It was not the first time Eadric had deserted Edmund. He had sided with Canute before, and some say his dastardly deed at Ashingdon may have been planned during that period. He may have 'rejoined' the King with the sole intention of betraying him at a convenient moment. Others suggest he merely did what he did when the going got tough and when he realised he would be better off serving the Danes again.

Most of the leading Anglo-Saxons were killed in the battle, though Edmund was lucky to escape with his life. It is said Eadric himself, on one occasion, deliberately killed a soldier who resembled the King. He only realised he had got the wrong man when he held up the head of his victim. Perhaps it is no surprise Eadric – because of his dubious allegiance – was unable to recognise the man he was supposed to be serving!

With most of his men lost, Edmund was forced to sign a treaty with Canute and the kingdom was divided between them. Edmund was allowed to rule Wessex, while Canute took control of the rest of the country. It was, one supposes, better than nothing. It was further agreed that whichever king died first, the other would then reign over the whole of England, their sons becoming heirs to the throne. Poor Edmund lived for just another six weeks and Canute became the undisputed first King of all England.

As for Eadric, he eventually received his comeuppance. At first he was rewarded for his services at Ashingdon, but it is believed he was later killed at the command of Canute. Presumably he had outlived his usefulness, or perhaps the canny Canute felt it was unwise to trust someone who had been so disloyal and treacherous in the past. The more romantic might prefer the fable that he was executed after beating Canute at chess!

Eadric already had a reputation for stopping at nothing to advance his own position, though his conduct at Ashingdon resulted in his most notorious act of treachery and he will forever be condemned as one of England's vilest traitors.

The famous battle – though other places in Essex have laid claim to being the site – is commemorated on the village sign at Ashingdon, near Rochford. Canute is believed to have returned to the scene of his triumph not long after to consecrate a church in memory of those that perished. It was built on the presumed site of the battle and remains a striking reminder of one of the country's most important events.

John Gates

Many important figures were involved in the attempt to put Lady Jane Grey on the throne of England in 1553. Sir John Gates, a former High Sheriff of Essex, was among the conspirators, and is believed to have been responsible for persuading Edward VI to name Lady Jane as his successor.

The once powerful Gates, who held many positions of high office under several monarchs, paid the ultimate price for his decision to support the Protestant cause. He was beheaded – a fate which was shared by the gentle and unfortunate Lady Jane herself the following year.

Beeleigh Abbey was home to conspirator Sir John Gates.

Poor Jane was merely a pawn in the whole affair. She was married to the son of the Duke of Northumberland, who, in an attempt to save the Protestant succession and safeguard his own future following the premature death of Edward, proclaimed his daughter-in-law Queen of England. Jane, the granddaughter of Henry VIII's sister Mary, was heir to the throne after Henry's daughters Mary and Elizabeth. Her reign famously lasted just nine days. The Duke of Northumberland was not a popular man and the people would not tolerate what was an illegal attempt to displace the rightful heir. The Duke was desperate to prevent Mary, a bigoted Catholic, from reigning. Despite hustling the innocent and reluctant Jane to London following Edward's death, the Duke failed to get the support he needed and the people rallied on the side of Mary Tudor. She entered the capital, accompanied by her half-sister Elizabeth, who had joined her at Wanstead, to be proclaimed Queen of England.

Lady Jane Grey had many ardent supporters in Essex because of her strong connections with the county. Few suffered the same fate as Gates, however. Some were imprisoned or had their estates seized, while others fled the country or made their peace with Mary Tudor.

Gates was not so lucky. He was charged with treason and executed at Tower Hill, a fate shared by the Duke of Northumberland. It was a dramatic fall from grace for Gates. He had been knighted by Edward VI, the country moving steadily towards Protestantism during his reign. Though his predecessor – Henry VIII – made the break from Catholicism, Henry still supported the doctrines of the Church of Rome. It was said Gates, despite his apparent ardent Protestantism – and much to the dismay of his own supporters – attended mass and recanted his Protestant faith before his execution. That would have pleased Mary Tudor more than anything. Her main aim on taking up the throne was to undo the Reformation and restore England to Rome. Some might suggest the country would have been better off if Lady Jane Grey had been allowed to rule. Mary's reign was one of the bloodiest, with some 300 Protestants put to death.

As for Gates, he is still remembered in Essex. One of his former homes in the county was Beeleigh Abbey. He acquired the property near Maldon following the Dissolution of the Monasteries as a reward for his services to Henry VIII. His headless ghost is said to still appear on the anniversary of his execution.

Thomas Howard, 4th Duke of Norfolk

Courtier Thomas Howard, 4th Duke of Norfolk, should have taken heed of the warning issued to him by Queen Elizabeth. Howard, the most powerful nobleman of his day, was playing a dangerous game. He was plotting to wed Mary, Queen of Scots in a bid to place her on the English throne and advance his own position. Elizabeth warned him to beware on what pillow he rested his head. However, Howard remained embroiled in the conspiracy to revive the fortunes of Mary Stuart, and his disloyalty to Elizabeth resulted in his execution for high treason in 1572. He was not the first of the famous Howard family to face the death penalty – his father suffered the same fate – but he was perhaps the most eminent, as at the time he was one of the Queen's favourites and held in such high regard within her court.

Howard was a powerful man, but was easily influenced. He allowed himself to be exploited by those with an even greater urge to put Mary on the English throne. It was others who suggested to him that a marriage between Scotland's fallen queen and England's greatest nobleman, a widower and the most eligible peer of the realm, could revive her fortunes and improve his own.

It was not the first time a match of this sort had been considered. Elizabeth herself had forwarded the name of Howard, along with other fellow courtiers, as a suitable husband for her cousin at one time. However, in 1567 Mary was forced to abdicate the Scottish throne and was accused of the murder of Lord Darnley, her second husband. Elizabeth could no longer afford to risk such a match, as the deposed Mary was a threat to her own throne now. She discovered Howard's intentions and ordered him to forget the idea. He could not. Even when he was briefly imprisoned in the Tower, he continued to secretly correspond with Mary and received letters declaring her love for him. Howard was still determined to marry a woman he had never even met. All the time, he was still pledging his undying loyalty to Elizabeth and she released him when persuaded his offences were not treasonable.

However, Howard lived at his London residence almost under house arrest and, in 1570, he was drawn into another conspiracy – the Ridolfi Plot. He reluctantly agreed to meet Roberto Ridolfi, an Italian papal agent who planned to depose Elizabeth, with the help of Catholic Spain, and put Mary on the English throne. Howard is said to have given verbal approval to his request for Spanish military assistance in the continuing drive to restore Mary to power. The plot was exposed and Howard was investigated. Amongst the incriminating evidence was a ciphered letter from Mary found under the doormat of his home.

It was the last straw for Elizabeth. He was again taken to the Tower and this time convicted of high treason, though he spent some four months awaiting his execution. Even now the betrayed Queen was still reluctant to see him executed as a traitor. Death warrants were signed and then revoked. Howard continued to write letters to Elizabeth from his prison cell, still declaring his loyalty, but it was in vain. The Queen eventually succumbed to the wishes of those around her, perhaps hoping the death of Howard would at least satisfy those baying for blood and even spare her fellow queen, who she did not wish to see die. However, it did neither and Mary, Queen of Scots also went on to suffer the same fate.

For Howard, it was a dramatic fall from grace. He had been, for a time, the only duke remaining in England. He was a man that seemed to have the world at his feet, but wanted more. His son – Thomas Howard, 1st Earl of Suffolk – inherited, via his mother, Audley End, near Saffron Walden, and was responsible for building one of the finest houses in England there.

Robert Devereux, 2nd Earl of Essex

You do not have to look far for examples of the impudence and tempestuousness of Robert Devereux, 2nd Earl of Essex. Few would even contemplate answering back a monarch, but Devereux famously drew his sword and was about to plunge it through the body of Queen Elizabeth during one disagreement. She had just slapped him in the face, however.

It was typical of their love-hate relationship. Fortunately on this occasion, a third party stepped in and stopped Devereux from doing something he would regret. However, the favourite of the Queen did go too far in the end and was eventually beheaded for treason in 1601.

Queen Elizabeth, as depicted at a Tolleshunt D'Arcy pub, is thought to have had a love-hate relationship with the rash and rebellious Earl of Essex.

If ever there was a case of hero to villain, it was that of Robert Devereux. He was a brave soldier, arguably the best in the land at the time, but he fell from grace in dramatic fashion, his relationship with Elizabeth ending in tragedy.

Robert was the son of Walter Devereux, 1st Earl of Essex. His father was also a controversial figure, responsible for committing acts of treachery and atrocities while serving in Ireland. He died in 1576, but there are suspicions he may have been poisoned by Robert Dudley, Earl of Leicester, who went on to marry Walter's widow, thus becoming the stepfather of Robert Devereux. Dudley was Lord Lieutenant of Essex in the 1580s. It was he who reputedly held the bridle reign of Elizabeth's horse when she made her most famous speech at Tilbury in anticipation of a feared attack from the Spanish Armada.

Robert Devereux took over the family home at Wanstead and also replaced his stepfather as the Queen's favourite. On the battlefield, he excelled himself. However, he was prone to disobeying Elizabeth's orders and they had many altercations, particularly over the problems in Ireland. She soon discovered he was a man that could not be ruled. Despite their differences, Devereux remained in her favour. Even after the famous slap in the face he received for turning his back on the Queen, the two eventually made their peace. Elizabeth was willing to endure his at times outrageous behaviour, probably because she felt she could not do without him.

However, there is only so much you can take sometimes and Devereux took things too far. In 1599, following in the footsteps of his father, he was sent to Ireland as Lord Lieutenant, for what turned out to be a very unsuccessful campaign. Devereux, physically sick and exhausted by the plucky resistance shown by the Irish, agreed a truce with the rebels. In truth, he was more concerned with what was happening in the royal court back at home. He was of the belief his opponents were poisoning the Queen against him. Angered by Elizabeth's damning letters over the way he had handled the Ireland campaign, Devereux deserted his post and returned home in an attempt to justify his actions to the monarch. However, it proved to be the last straw. Elizabeth was not impressed and he was deprived of his offices. It was the beginning of the end for Devereux. He was confined to house arrest and was ruined, both politically and financially.

In desperation, Devereux began to plot a way back to power. He was convinced the Queen had become a puppet to some of his court rivals, who he believed were now traitors because of their willingness to deal with the Spanish, the old enemy, who Devereux had gained such distinction fighting against. He was of the opinion they could never be trusted.

The conspiracy was poorly planned, which was perhaps typical of a man known for his rashness. By now, Devereux was a broken figure, in poor health, a shadow of his former self. The rebellion was doomed from the start. However, with a few hundred loyal followers, Devereux marched into London in a bid to stir the people to revolt. Though some carried swords, it was said they had few weapons and no body armour. Even some of his own men deserted him. The end was quick in coming. Devereux surrendered and was eventually executed at the Tower of London after being found guilty of treason. Rather ungallantly, it is believed he implicated his own sister – Penelope – in the plot, though she, despite his betrayal, never incriminated him.

There is a bizarre footnote concerning the death of Devereux involving a man named Wiseman of Great Canfield, near Great Dunmow, who perhaps did not live up to his name. Devereux is said to have written a final letter pleading to Elizabeth for mercy, but Wiseman did not deliver it on time. On learning his master had been beheaded – as a form of self-punishment – he vowed to never again sleep in a bed. And so, for the remaining 45 years of his life, the distraught Wiseman is said to have slept in a couch carved out of the trunk of a tree.

George Eliot

Even when he was due to face execution, gentle John Payne only had words of forgiveness for the man who betrayed him. The much-loved priest said of informer of Catholics George Eliot: 'I forgive his monstrous wickedness and defy his malicious inventions.'

Both Payne and Eliot had lived under the same roof at Ingatestone Hall, home of the Petres, which became a major centre for Catholicism in Essex. The Petre family supported Catholics throughout the reign of a number of monarchs, but never more so than when the Protestant Queen Elizabeth came to the throne. Though Elizabeth was not in the same league as Mary I when it came to prosecuting 'heretics', her laws were still harsh. Priests and those that sheltered them were playing a dangerous game.

While Sir William Petre kept his faith pretty much to himself, his wife was a devout papist and well known as one that would not accept the newly-established Church of England. Lady Petre, following the death of her husband, harboured many seminary priests, and secret services were regularly held at her home. Visitors today can still see the priest holes.

Payne resided at Ingatestone Hall for many years, in the guise of an estate steward. He was first arrested in 1577 and briefly imprisoned before moving abroad. However, Payne returned and, in 1581, he was arrested again, this time after being betrayed by Eliot, an apostate Catholic – now turned spy – who was a servant at Ingatestone Hall.

A trumped-up charge of plotting to dethrone the Queen was laid before Payne. There was a lengthy investigation before his trial. Payne was convicted on Eliot's evidence that he had uttered treasonable words against the Queen while at Ingatestone. Though he may have been guilty of saying mass, there was no plot to unseat Elizabeth in a bid to restore the Catholic religion, and his innocence was generally accepted by most, if not by the court. Payne suffered much during the eight months he spent in the Tower of London awaiting his fate. He was regularly tortured on the rack, but would not denounce his faith and conform to the new Church of England. However, even on the scaffold at Chelmsford in 1582, he declared that 'his feet did never tread, his hands did never write, nor his wit ever invent any treason against Her Majesty'.

Payne was condemned to suffer the death of a traitor, to be hanged, drawn and quartered. So loved was he that the crowd begged the hangman to ensure Payne was dead before cutting him down to spare him any further agony. And so Payne became the only Catholic priest to be executed in Essex during the reign of Queen Elizabeth. For his martyrdom, he was canonised in 1970 and a Roman Catholic secondary school in Chelmsford is now named in his honour.

As for Eliot, he was also involved in the arrest of an even more famous Catholic, alerting the authorities to the whereabouts of Jesuit Edmund Campion, who was executed in 1581. Eliot was not a nice man and made money out of betraying those of a faith he himself had once observed. Among Catholic circles he was viewed as a despicable traitor and better known to them as George 'Judas' Eliot.

Chapter Eight

Witches

Essex has always been known as witch country. Hundreds were prosecuted for witchcraft in the sixteenth and seventeenth centuries. The village witch could be blamed for anything, including failed crops or even a miscarriage. If there was no obvious explanation, superstitious parishioners would more than likely point the finger at the eccentric hag that had a wart on the end of her nose.

Of course – with scientific and medical knowledge still in its infancy – many did rely on ancient charms and spells in search of cures. The man at the centre of witchcraft in Essex was not a witch himself. However, few can doubt he was a more loathsome individual than any of the poor souls he so cruelly put to death during one of the most shameful periods in the country's history.

Matthew Hopkins

There were probably no more witches in Essex and East Anglia than anywhere else in the country. It was just that this particular part of the world was home to the self-proclaimed Witchfinder General – Matthew Hopkins.

The counties of Essex and Suffolk had the highest number of convictions for witchcraft in England, while the seventeenth century

Matthew Hopkins – the notorious persecutor of witches.

saw the greatest number of trials. Hopkins is the reason for this. He made it his mission to seek out 'witches' and, in doing so, was responsible for the deaths of hundreds, mostly ignorant and vulnerable women. Hopkins was not the only one to set himself up as a witch-hunter in order to profit from the hysteria caused by the increase in the practice of witchcraft, though he certainly became not only the most famous in Essex, but the whole of the country.

Little is known about the early life of Hopkins or even the end of it. It is thought he died of consumption in his late twenties, though some are of the belief he got his comeuppance and was executed after he himself was accused of being a sorcerer. Matthew Hopkins may have become a mass murderer, but his childhood gave little indication of the path he would take. He was the son of James Hopkins, a Puritan minister at Great Wenham, just over the Essex border in Suffolk. His father is thought to have also been a landowner, so the childhood of the young Matthew would have probably been better than most of his age. He was likely to have had a good education and a solid upbringing.

What made this son of a holy man go off the rails will perhaps never be known. Perhaps he sought some sort of celebrity status. It is believed he was a humble clerk and may have also been a failed solicitor before turning to the pursuit of rounding up witches.

Hopkins may have carried out his relentless search for witches for religious purposes. His father was a Puritan after all, but most historians are of the opinion that money was his only motivation. Despite his callous regard for human life, one has to admit that Hopkins must have been a fine entrepreneur. He took advantage of the paranoia of the day. The Civil War was nearing its end and the country, now under Parliamentarian control, was in chaos. By 1645, the year in which Hopkins began his sordid trade, the Royalists were a spent force. The Puritan influence in England was never as strong as it was between 1645 and the Restoration of the monarchy in 1660.

Hopkins had Puritanism on his side. The evil practice of witchcraft was much maligned by God-fearing Puritans. With the Royalists almost out of the way, it became a new common enemy, something else to unite communities. Hopkins seized the opportunity and, with the country still in chaos with regard to governance, there was no long arm of the law to put an end to his barbarism.

Hopkins' reign of terror did not last long, barely two years, but certainly more than 200 people (maybe many more) died at his hands. It also made him a wealthy man. Hopkins would give advance warning he was to visit a certain place. He would charge a consultation fee and for an initial survey. Then he was on commission. It was certainly in his interests to round up witches, as he was paid for every one that was tried and sentenced.

It all meant that innocent women, some of whom never even had any interest in the occult, were singled out. It has to be remembered that the country was still very superstitious and Hopkins played on this fact. The witches he rounded up were usually the more vulnerable people in society, those of a poor education who could not defend themselves. It was easy to accuse somebody of being a witch, but Hopkins had to prove it. He would use psychological torture to extract a confession. The accused would often be deprived of food and sleep for up to three days and, in desperation, on the point of madness, usually gave in. There was also the threat of the infamous swimming test. The unfortunate woman – for it was more often females – would be thrown into the village pond. If she floated, she would be declared one of Satan's own. On the flip side, if she drowned, she would at least go to her grave being declared innocent!

Hopkins was not an Essex man, but he certainly died in the county. It is not known when exactly he settled in Mistley, near Manningtree, but it was some time in the 1640s. This is where his reign of terror began. His first victim was a one-legged woman named Elizabeth Clarke. A local tailor had blamed his wife's

Matthew Hopkins is said to have plotted his upcoming crusades at the Thorn Inn.

illness on witchcraft, believing Elizabeth to be the perpetrator. He started to circulate rumours that she was responsible and the word, in such a close-knit community, did not take long to spread. Elizabeth had a reputation for being a nasty woman and her own mother had also been executed for witchcraft. She was perhaps the obvious target at which to vent his fury.

Elizabeth admitted keeping company with witches and went on to incriminate others. Under interrogation, she even confessed to having intercourse with Satan, and is reputed to have turned to Hopkins and declared that the Evil One was 'a properer [*sic*] man than yourself'! It seems Elizabeth was at the very least a feisty character. Her other 'crimes' were keeping a number of familiars. These were supernatural spirits that appeared in animal form, working as agents of Satan. Of course, they would be regarded as no more than pets in this day and age. Familiars lived on blood suckled from their owners. Elizabeth is said to have had three unnatural teats for the purpose. One of Elizabeth's familiars, according to Hopkins, was a greyhound that reputedly transformed itself into a child with no head on one occasion.

Ironically, Hopkins also owned a greyhound, though his beast was, of course, just an ordinary pet.

Elizabeth was hanged at Chelmsford, along with a dozen or so other witches from Manningtree and the surrounding area. Four more suffered the same fate in Manningtree itself. Among them was Anne West of Lawford, though her daughter Rebecca, also accused of witchcraft, somehow escaped punishment. Some historians have suggested that she gave detailed evidence against her fellow Manningtree witches – including her mother – in return for her own freedom. Hopkins is known to have visited her in prison at Colchester Castle on more than one occasion. Perhaps he made a deal with her, though some have suggested they may have even had an affair. Certainly, she vanished without trace.

Hopkins turned his attention to Suffolk, the place of his birth, following the executions at Chelmsford and Manningtree, and his list of victims continued to grow ever longer. It is believed Hopkins had a secret office at the Thorn Inn in Mistley. In fact, it is said his ghost still haunts the establishment. Some believe he used the office to plan his forthcoming crusades. It has also been suggested he lived at the inn, while others claim his home stood close by at The Green.

Hopkins believed he had the blessing of those in power to carry out his cleansing of East Anglia, including the Pope. As mentioned earlier, superstition was rife and witchcraft was believed to be the work of Satan. Hopkins did not work alone. He had at least two assistants. John Stearne, a devout Puritan, seemed to be acting on religious motives and genuinely believed his mission was the work of God. Unlike Hopkins, money was not thought to be his incentive. Mary Phillips was possibly a midwife and entrusted with the job of searching for deformities or unnatural marks on the bodies of Hopkins' accused victims. The trio were known as 'the three unspotted lambs of the Lord'.

Much of what we know about the reign of Hopkins and Stearne comes from the pens of both men. Both wrote accounts of their work. Hopkins penned *The Discovery of Witches* as almost a defence to his actions, at a time when Parliament was perhaps starting to think his work was not the will of God after all. It was published in the year of his death.

Some say Matthew Hopkins met his own fate at the Hopping Bridge in Manningtree.

Stearne outlived Hopkins and reported that the Witchfinder General died of consumption. The parish records at Mistley only state the time of Hopkins' death. He died in 1647. There are some who claim he got his just deserts and was executed after being accused of witchcraft himself. One theory is that he had to undergo the swimming test. This practice was now illegal so it would have been unofficial. Perhaps the villagers had had enough of their self-proclaimed Witchfinder General and took the law into their own hands. Some say Hopkins was 'swam' at the Hopping Bridge, not far from his Mistley home. He might have drowned, but could have also died as a result of the test, his consumption becoming worse following the ordeal of being thrown into the freezing water. It is all conjecture.

Hopkins was buried at Mistley Heath, possibly in an unmarked grave. The church itself no longer stands anyway, so we will never know the true fate of one of the most infamous characters of the English Civil War and a true villain of Essex.

Agnes Waterhouse & Elizabeth Francis

Every witch should have a cat. Agnes Waterhouse of Hatfield Peverel, near Witham, supposedly used her feline friend to bump off a neighbour, but it was at a cost. In 1566, she became the first resident of Essex and England to be hanged following a trial for witchcraft.

Agnes was not the first to discover the cat had supernatural powers. It belonged to a fellow Hatfield Peverel resident, Elizabeth Francis. She was to follow Agnes to the gallows.

It is said Elizabeth gave Agnes her cat in return for a cake. She told her about its powers and claimed it could do anything. Elizabeth is reputed to have used it to kill Andrew Byles, a wealthy man who refused to do the honourable thing in marrying Elizabeth after getting her pregnant. His rejection left her fuming. In revenge, using the evil powers of her cat, she is said to have first wrecked his goods, probably his crops, and then aborted the baby she was carrying by concocting a lethal potion of wild herbs and probably other less inviting ingredients. Byles was himself killed via the possessed cat touching his body.

It seems Elizabeth was determined to find a husband, but, when she did, she soon tired of him. Christopher Francis had, unlike Byles, agreed to marry his seducer after she again became pregnant. Doing the honourable thing did not work in his favour either. After the unwanted baby was killed via the cat, Elizabeth soon discovered she did not need a husband after all. She commanded her cat to make him lame. The familiar did this by changing into a toad and jumping into one of his boots. The disease in his foot spread to the rest of his body and he died after becoming paralysed.

Neighbour Agnes, on receiving the cat from Elizabeth, first tried out its powers by dispatching the farm animals of residents who had angered her. She then used it to bump off a neighbour. Agnes also confessed to using witchcraft to see off her own husband as well.

Both Agnes Waterhouse and Elizabeth Francis stood trial at Chelmsford. The daughter of Agnes also joined them in the dock – Joan Waterhouse was still a teenager. She denied everything at first, but later admitted she too had experimented with the cat. She had seen what it was capable of doing under her mother's command and decided to have a go herself, keen to punish a neighbour who had refused to give her some bread and cheese. She told the trial that she summoned the familiar, which on this occasion appeared in the guise of a large dog. The animal seemed not to want to co-operate, though it was not long before an evil dog with horns paid a visit to the neighbour – a child of just twelve – who had been the target of Joan's wrath.

It was not only the testimony of Joan that put paid to her mother. Agnes' own confession that the cat had suckled her was proof enough for most people during those dark times. The reward for a familiar in seeing off unwanted husbands, and other unfortunate creatures, was usually a drop of blood from its owner. Being suckled by familiars was a sure sign the person was a witch.

Agnes pleaded guilty and was sentenced to death; she was hanged. Her daughter Joan was found not guilty, while Elizabeth somehow escaped the noose and was only imprisoned for a year. However, she did not learn her lesson and was soon back to her old ways. After inflicting revenge on another neighbour who had been less than generous with their harvest, Elizabeth found herself in the dock again. This time she was found guilty of murder by witchcraft and hanged.

Ursley Kempe

You do not want to offend a witch. Victims of witches, as we have already seen, were usually people who had insulted them, or refused the offer of a gift or service.

Ursley Kempe became the focus of a notorious witch-hunt in the village of St Osyth, near Clacton-on-Sea – a place associated with witchcraft. After carrying out punishment on an ungrateful neighbour, Ursley found herself one of more than a dozen people accused of witchcraft in what was one of the largest trials of its kind in England.

The famous St Osyth incident prompted Reginald Scot to pen *The Discovery of Witchcraft* in 1584, a book that attempted to counter the opinion that witches were everywhere. Scot was a sceptic and blamed those investigating the cult for its growth. He was ahead of his time, for the work was written long before the infamous Witchfinder General Matthew Hopkins had created mass hysteria with his unrelenting persecution of witches in East Anglia.

The man responsible for bringing Ursley Kempe to book was not in the same league as Hopkins, but he certainly made it his mission to clean up St Osyth and the surrounding area. Brian Darcy was the local squire and a judge. He used Ursley to bring other witches to book and, in the mould of Hopkins, was perhaps just as much the villain as the defendants standing before him.

Ursley Kempe, unlike many accused of witchcraft, appeared to be more liked than some of her contemporaries, at least at first. She had a reputation for being able to heal sick children. On one occasion when the mother of a little boy with a fever was close to despair, Ursley offered her services free of charge and successfully healed the child. The mother was an employee of the lord of the manor, Darcy. When she was about to give birth to another child, he suggested she sought help from Ursley, such was her reputation and the fact she had come to her aid in the past. However, the mother suspected Ursley to be a witch and, though probably glad of her help when she was desperate and had no-one else to call on, this time snubbed her. Ursley was much offended and, as we have discovered, it was not a good idea to upset a witch. The mother's newborn baby fell from its cot and died. The mother herself also became ill. Ursley offered to heal her, but this time she was not willing to offer her services for free. The mother still agreed to let her help her and is said to have been relieved of her pain. However, when she refused to pay Ursley her fee, claiming she was too poor, the pain returned. Now convinced Ursley was a witch – and perhaps in a bid for revenge – the mother informed Darcy. In the meantime, another resident had also accused Ursley of making her son ill, the witch reputedly putting a curse on her because she had been less than neighbourly.

With village gossip rife, Darcy soon became interested and decided to question Ursley. She at first denied his claims that she possessed an understanding of witchcraft. However, Darcy was a clever man and began to win her trust. Ursley soon admitted that she had received some healing from a witch many years ago when she had sought a cure for a particular ailment, the chief ingredient being dung from a hog. The remedy – however distasteful it may have sounded – proved successful, prompting Ursley to set up as a herbal witch herself. She was of the belief a witch had once also cursed her and that she would only cast off the spell by doing good works.

Ursley soon revealed everything to Darcy, due to an offer of clemency from the cunning squire. She revealed she owned four familiars, which had been responsible for the punishment of the mother who had shunned her when giving birth. Still believing she would be spared, Ursley also incriminated others involved in witchcraft.

Darcy questioned more villagers, threatening them with the noose if they did not co-operate. The village became hysterical. Rumours continued to abound. People would accuse their neighbour or even family members, possibly in a bid to deflect any possible guilt from themselves. There was utter panic.

The accused residents of St Osyth and neighbouring villages were put on trial. The witches were blamed for causing all sorts of problems, from turning bread mouldy, to possessing familiars and using them to make people ill. Witnesses were often young children, probably relishing the chance to be in the spotlight. It is more than probable many were a little too liberal with the truth, unaware the fate of people in the village, possibly even their own mother, was in their hands. The illegitimate son of Ursley, believed to be no more than eight, was one of those who gave evidence against her.

It is believed only two of the accused were hanged, one of those being Ursley Kempe. The others were discharged, acquitted or sentenced to death, but eventually reprieved. Despite Scot's book, people only became more suspicious of witchcraft and many more unfortunate folk were brought to 'justice' in the years to follow.

Old Mother Moore

Sarah Moore, better known as Old Mother Moore, was the bane of the Essex coast. Nineteenth-century sailors lived in fear of the notorious 'sea witch' of Leigh-on-Sea.

She would sit on the wharf and see off those about to set sail. However, she was the last person the superstitious sailors wanted to bump in to, as it must have cost them a small fortune over time.

It is not difficult to imagine Old Mother Moore terrifying sailors on the quay at Leigh-on-Sea.

Sarah would insist they bought a 'fair wind' from her. She is said to have had the power to control the weather. Those who refused her 'insurance' would be in for a rough time at sea. Seamen were convinced she had the power to conjure up a storm at will. Departing sailors thought it was a cheap price to pay in order to prevent her wrecking their fishing or doing much worse.

There was no doubt many sailors were scared of Old Mother Moore. They became very nervous when approaching her and did their best not to cause her any distress. She was the archetypal witch, at least in appearance. She is said to have possessed a harelip and hooked nose. Some said she was unattractive and appeared to be dirty.

According to a romantic tale that has passed through the generations, Sarah died in dramatic circumstances. There is a legend that she was responsible for a storm in the Thames Estuary that she had whipped up in revenge for a skipper that had dared to mock her. The young seaman was new to the area and unaware of her fearsome reputation. He had refused to pay for a fair wind and even had the audacity to laugh at her as his vessel left Leigh-on-Sea. He soon changed his tune. While at sea, the wind suddenly dropped and a sense of calm followed. It was definitely the lull before the storm.

Dark clouds began to gather and it was not long before he and his crew found themselves in the midst of a tempest. It had seemingly stemmed from nowhere and, as the thunder cracked and lightning flashed, the crew became convinced it was the work of one person – the sea witch of Leigh-on-Sea. It appears they also managed to convince their skipper too, though he may have already been regretting his decision to refuse to pay Old Mother Moore. He is said to have grabbed an axe and declared, 'I'll kill her.' He rushed below deck and struck the bow of the ship three times. As quick as the storm had flared up, it ceased. The sun broke through the clouds and calm returned. When the crew came in sight of Leigh-on-Sea, they saw the figure of a woman slumped on the waterside. It was Old Mother Moore. She was dead. On closer examination, three mysterious gashes were found on her forehead.

It is believed Old Mother Moore was born at the end of the eighteenth century. Apart from terrorising sailors, landlubbers feared her just as much. She was accused of putting spells on newborn babies for no other reason than envy, having lost her own sons to cholera in 1849. The experience seemingly turned her into a bitter and cruel woman.

It was said her unusual facial features – the harelip and hooked nose – would appear on the new-born children of the mothers who had upset Sarah. She was reputedly also able to kill people with fire and flash sparks from her eyes. The deaths of a number of infants may have been her work, according to legend.

Old Mother Moore was not unique. There were numerous sea witches operating on the Essex coast, all eager to profit from sailors, a notoriously suspicious breed of people at the best of times.

George Pickingill

The village of Canewdon has always been considered the centre of witchcraft in Essex. It still is today. Of course, few current residents believe in the legend that the village will always be home to six (some say nine) witches so long as the church tower

Canewdon village sign pictures a witch flying her broomstick, indicating that it was once considered the centre of witchcraft in Essex.

stands. According to tradition, every time a stone falls from the tower, a witch will die and another will take its place. However, some say it is when the last witch of Canewdon dies that the tower of St Nicholas' Church will collapse.

George Pickingill was the most famous witch of Canewdon, a village north of Rochford. It was said he only had to whistle for the other witches in the village to appear at their doors. Pickingill lived most of his life in the nineteenth century, when – perhaps fortunately for him – witches were not being persecuted to the extent of previous centuries. That is not to say he was not feared and mistrusted. It is believed he possessed an evil eye and could make someone unwell by just looking at them. Villagers would do their best to avoid his glance and certainly did not want to upset him. It is said that he did not need any money. Superstitious neighbours provided for his needs. Farmers supplied him with everything he could want in order to prevent him from putting a spell on their crops. He was supposedly partial to a beer, and residents soon discovered buying him a glass of his favourite tipple

Some say the parish church will collapse when the last witch in Canewdon disappears.

could avert the threat of a curse. People would quicken their step when they passed his cottage and few dared to look inside.

Pickingill was a farm labourer by trade, but during harvest time, he would sit back with a beer and let his imps carry out the hard work in the fields. He is said to have had the gift of healing and people would also come to him, if they dared, whenever something was lost, as another of his gifts was being able to locate stolen or misplaced property.

Pickingill was born at Hockley in 1816. He lived to an old age. His death and subsequent funeral proved to be quite an event. On his deathbed, he is reported to have told people that he would reveal his powers one final time after he had left this world. Reputed to be able to bewitch machines, animals seemingly fell under his spell too. It is said that when the funeral procession arrived at the church, one of the horses, for no apparent reason, broke away from the shafts and bolted, much to everyone's amazement. There was a strong belief that certain people had the power to stop or start horses at will. It seems Pickingill still had this gift even beyond the grave. Others spoke of lightning striking Pickingill's cottage on the night he passed away.

There are many myths surrounding the life and death of George Pickingill. However, there are no recorded details of his 'crimes'. It is all just hearsay. Despite this, he was not mourned and many treated his death as a relief. Of course, with his demise another witch would have taken his place, though they would not have been in quite the same mould as this true legend of Canewdon.

Further evidence of the belief in one witch being replaced by another in Canewdon can be found in the tale of a local blacksmith. On his deathbed, in severe pain, he is said to have cast his eye all about the room as though he was searching for something. Suddenly a mouse appeared and the blacksmith begged his wife to take it. She refused, for she knew what her husband was asking of her. Legend has it that when one witch dies, their power is passed on to the next witch via a familiar or imp, in this case a mouse. It was normal for a witch to want to pass on their familiars to a relative. Fortunately for the blacksmith, his compassionate daughter took the creature, a sign that she was willing to accept familiars into her care, and subsequently replace him as one of the witches of Canewdon. Finally free of his burden, the blacksmith was able to die in peace.

Cunning Murrell

Witchcraft was not looked upon as such a great evil in the nineteenth century. In fact, even the word 'witch' was replaced by much more presentable names, such as 'cunning man' or 'wise woman'.

There is no doubt James Murrell of Hadleigh would have been labelled a witch if he had lived at another time, however. He was just fortunate that witchcraft was no longer deemed to be such villainy, and he could even profit from still-superstitious people who came to him in need of assistance. He became a sort of doctor, vet, fortune-teller and even psychiatrist.

Murrell was the most famous cunning man of Essex and maybe England. He was born in Rochford and claimed to be the seventh son of a seventh son. He settled in Hadleigh in the early part of the nineteenth century, setting up a business as a shoemaker.

However, his interests lay elsewhere, particularly in chemistry. Every successful witch should be able to create a potion or two, and Cunning Murrell certainly did that. He was famed for his magic concoctions, and would often be seen at night on the nearby downs collecting herbs for his spells.

Murrell's reputation grew. People came from far and wide for his help. His gifts included being able to cure both people and animals of illness, but also to bewitch them. He could break spells and drive away demons. He could even locate hidden treasure.

Like all witches in days gone by, it is not really known how great his powers actually were. Many witches played upon people's superstitions and naivety, profiting from their fears. Murrell would fuel the rumours and gossip surrounding him in order to enhance his reputation further. He relied upon his reputation. It was the key to his success. His cottage was furnished with everything a man of mystery should have. Herbs hung from the ceiling and there was a human skull on a table. A bucket of oily fluid was used as a sort of crystal ball to help locate lost property. His secret papers, consisting of spells, calculations and notes, were kept in a huge chest. Murrell was certainly a showman but also a very clever man. He meticulously kept notes on all the villagers. When a resident came for a consultation, Murrell would know all about them and they would be amazed when he revealed details about themselves that they thought only they would know. The information proved invaluable in solving problems and telling fortunes.

Some would argue that Murrell's act was all a con, but it is said that he only charged people what they could afford. And the people could not get enough of him. The post office serving Hadleigh is said to have handled three times as many letters addressed to him as anyone else in the town put together. Murrell would have made a lot of money, but then he did have a large family to support. It is said he fathered up to twenty children, even if many probably died in childbirth or at a young age.

Murrell had a strange appearance, which was probably to his advantage. He wore circular-rimmed glasses made of iron and walked with his arms behind his back, his head held high in the air. It is said he could travel great distances at night while gathering ingredients for his potions. Some believed he could even fly through the air or be in two places at the same time.

It was Murrell's potions that attracted most attention. His iron 'witch bottles' used for breaking spells became legendary. They contained a mixture of blood, urine, hair, nail cuttings, herbs and pins. The bottles were sealed and placed in the fire, so that they gave off a hissing sound as they burnt, before becoming so hot that they exploded. Gullible clients watching it all in the dark room, the only light coming from the flames, the only sound a hypnotising hissing from the bottle, would have probably been terrified.

On one occasion, a young girl came to Murrell for help after being cursed by a gypsy. She had started to run on all fours and would bark like a dog. Murrell produced one of his famous iron bottles and placed it on the fire. As the hissing increased, there was a frantic knock on the door and a desperate voice shouted, 'Stop! You're killing me.'

It was only when the bottle finally exploded that the shouting and knocking at the door ceased. The stranger had seemingly fled, but the next day the body of the gypsy was found a few miles away – the corpse badly burnt. At least, or so the story goes, the young girl was cured of her unusual affliction, even if it was at the expense of the unfortunate gypsy.

Murrell is believed to have died in 1860. He supposedly predicted the exact date and time of his death to the hour. No other cunning man or wise woman in Essex ever gained the same reputation as that of James Murrell. His ghost is said to still haunt Daws Heath in its relentless search for herbs.

Sadly, or perhaps not, none of his infamous iron witch bottles survive. The forger who produced the bottles reported that the last remaining one following Murrell's death fell into the hands of one of the cunning man's sons – and he reputedly blew up a client's wall with it!

Chapter Nine

Miscellaneous Villains

Acts of villainy come in all different forms. Sometimes it is not possible to place a villain into one particular bracket. Their 'crime' can be almost unique or they can, of course, be responsible for committing more than one.

The following miscreants deserve a mention for being among the best (or perhaps worst) of the rest of Essex villains.

The Vikings

There have been many unwelcome visitors to Essex. Indeed, the course of British history has been shaped by those that have invaded our shores and then settled here. However, the Romans, Saxons and Normans might be viewed as saints compared to the Danes and their fellow Scandinavian raiders.

The most famous Viking invasion in Essex occurred at Maldon in 991. It was one of the most epic events in the county's history, though its renown is probably more due to a piece of Old English literature. *The Battle of Maldon* is a poem of which only a fragment survives. It is one of the oldest surviving English poems, recounting the story of the heroic death of Byrhtnoth at the hands of the Vikings.

Byrhtnoth was an Essex giant. It is believed he was a mere three inches from being 7ft tall. He was of a grand age when he stood up to the pillaging Vikings, and this Anglo-Saxon ealdorman – though he lost his life – has become a hero of Essex and England.

The Vikings were ravaging the East Anglia coastline and made their way up the Blackwater to set up camp at Northey Island, just off the Maldon coastline. Byrhtnoth assembled his army on the mainland in anticipation of the battle. The odds favoured the invaders, as they were blessed with greater numbers, but the brave locals did have one thing

Maldon remembers brave Byrhtnoth, but he was unable to see off the Vikings.

in their favour – the tidal causeway that led from the mainland to the island. The Vikings would have to cross it to reach Byrhtnoth and his loyal band of followers. Because of its narrowness, the Anglo-Saxons would have been able to pick them off one by one as they crossed almost in single file. Unfortunately, for whatever reason, they did not take up the opportunity.

Incredibly, the Vikings were allowed to cross unchallenged and set up battle lines on the mainland itself. Some suggest it was a mistake on Byrhtnoth's part to allow them to advance unhindered. It has been suggested he was too complacent, though the more romantic prefer to think it was Byrhtnoth's sense of chivalry, his desire for fair play, which permitted the challengers to cross the causeway. Byrhtnoth was an old warrior, a symbol of Saxon honour and virtue, so it is perhaps quite conceivable that he could not bring himself to attack in almost cold blood, to slaughter men that had little chance of protecting themselves.

The invading Vikings crossed the causeway from Northey Island to reach the mainland unchallenged.

Of course, once allowed to form their army on the mainland, the Vikings – who perhaps did not abide by the same chivalrous code of conduct – wasted no time in defeating the honourable Byrhtnoth and his followers. The Vikings were simply unstoppable. Without any hope of victory, Byrhtnoth and his brave troops still put up a fight and the raiders, even with the odds in their favour, suffered greatly. It is said they could scarcely manage their ships after the battle.

Perhaps Byrhtnoth was foolish, but one cannot question his bravery. His statue now stands at Maldon, while the battle is commemorated in a stained-glass window at St Mary's Church. The tidal causeway still connects Maldon to Northey Island, another visible reminder of the most famous Viking invasion in Essex.

Certainly, the county of Essex suffered much at the hands of the marauding and pillaging Danes. Their cruelty is perhaps summed up by the story of Osyth, thought to be the daughter and wife of Saxon kings. She was a prioress, who paid the ultimate price for her faith. When the invading Vikings attempted to get the nuns to renounce their Christian beliefs, Osyth defiantly stepped forward to confront them. She was beheaded on the spot, the leader of the Vikings furious a woman had dared to humiliate him. It is said Osyth picked up her severed head and calmly took it to the chapel before dropping dead. There are many versions of the legend, but it is generally believed this Christian martyr was later canonised, the village of St Osyth, close to Clacton-on-Sea, taking its present name from her. Part of St Osyth's Priory still stands.

The author Sabine Baring-Gould, who lived on Mersea Island for a spell, referred to the incident in his novel *Mehalah*, which is set in the county. One of the characters claims Osyth had a sister, who also suffered at the hands of the Danes. It is said she was brought back to Mersea – where the Vikings had a camp – by the twin brothers who had been responsible for the death of Osyth. They possessed one heart and soul between them. What one desired, so did the other. The sister was as pretty as Osyth and the twin chiefs quarrelled over who was to have her. The brothers' love for each other turned to jealousy and they fought a furious battle before both succumbed to their wounds. After their deaths, the Danes drew their ship to a small hill just above The Strood on Mersea Island, placing in the hold of the vessel each dead brother either side of the still-alive maiden. A mountain of earth was piled on top of the ship and all three were buried. In the book, Elijah Rebow tells the heroine Mehalah, that during a full moon, the two brothers rise from their grave and passers-by can hear them still fighting deep inside the barrow.

St Osyth's Priory, scene of another atrocity at the hands of the Vikings.

In 870, the Vikings also famously razed Barking Abbey, one of the richest in Essex at the time, burning to death all the nuns within the walls of their own church. It was just another act of atrocity by arguably the worst of all the invaders to have settled on our shores.

John Hawkwood

You have to have done something bad to be labelled 'the Devil incarnate'.

Soldier Sir John Hawkwood, perhaps the country's most famous mercenary, did indeed do just that. Though historians recognise that he was a great military leader, his ruthless massacring of innocent people will always overshadow his achievements on the battlefields of France and, in particular, his adopted country of Italy.

It was the shameful slaughter of the people of Cesena in 1377, on behalf of the Pope, that so blotted Hawkwood's copybook. Not even women or children were spared. There is one story in which he is accused of cutting a captive nun in half in order to

Mercenary Sir John Hawkwood is still remembered in Sible Hedingham.

stop two of his soldiers arguing over who should have her. There are many myths surrounding the life of this incredible soldier of fortune, but there is little doubt Hawkwood could be responsible for such a savage act, and there are numerous tales of his cruelty as a mercenary. The Diabolical Englishman, as he is now sometimes called, had no qualms about making a fortune out of war. He himself once declared that peace would ruin him.

Hawkwood left Essex to fight in the English army at the start of the Hundred Years' War. It is believed he distinguished himself during the battles at Crécy and Poitiers, before being knighted by Edward III.

Like many soldiers, Hawkwood was left in limbo when peace with France was declared. Instead of returning to England and an uncertain future, he decided to use his military talents to bring in a wage, becoming a mercenary commander. It was in Italy where he spent most of his life, fighting for whoever was willing to pay for his services. His White Company, one of a number of freelance troops in operation throughout Europe at the time, had a fine reputation and Hawkwood was in great demand. It meant he amassed a considerable fortune. He acquired land and property, sometimes by conquest, or sometimes as payment, or even as a bribe. His company was also accused of much pillaging, something usually undertaken when there was not much work about. There is no doubt, however, that his biggest crime was the sacking of Cesena, though he is said to have deserted his papal employer after the event, which suggests that even Hawkwood believed he had gone too far on this occasion. Throughout his career, he had no problem switching allegiance, choosing the side that best suited him.

Hawkwood is believed to have fought well into old age. Some say he may have been in his early seventies when he took part in his final battle, helping his adopted Florence to a great victory against the odds. He became a hero to that particular city, and back in England too. Hawkwood is even depicted on the village sign at Sible Hedingham, near Halstead. It is thought his body was returned to his former home following his death. However, the atrocities committed at Cesena and elsewhere, have also earned him a reputation as a ruthless barbarian who profited out of the

The grand tomb of Richard Rich – the 'worst' Briton of the sixteenth century.

horrors of war. Catherine of Siena, who was later declared a saint, was among those that condemned one of the greatest, but controversial, military leaders of his time.

Richard Rich

Richard Rich had the unenviable distinction of being named the worst Briton of the sixteenth century in a BBC poll. He was responsible for so many and varied acts of treachery and evil, it is difficult to place him in a particular bracket of villains. However, it was perhaps his betrayal of a man who became a saint – Sir Thomas More – that has earned him the greatest infamy. Despite his loyal service to the Crown and charitable acts, particularly towards the end of his life, his role in securing the conviction of More has left an indelible mark in an already black copybook.

Rich's rise to power had much to do with another Essex resident. He was a friend of Sir Thomas Audley, who replaced More as Lord Chancellor. Audley became a powerful patron, appointing Rich to the role of Solicitor General in 1533. Rich became responsible for the prosecution of those who opposed the royal supremacy, Henry VIII's idea of the monarch being head of the Church. Bishop John Fisher and More were Rich's most famous 'victims', both being convicted and executed for treason. Rich interrogated both in the Tower of London. He is believed to have tricked Fisher into gaining the necessary evidence to incriminate him. As for More, a fellow lawyer, it is said Rich falsely testified at the trial – that during his interrogation More had explicitly denied the King was the legitimate head of the Church.

Audley – another Essex 'villain' – was also criticised for his handling of the trials of both More and Fisher, which were said to have made a mockery of justice. He was accused of allowing the convictions to rest on the unsubstantiated testimonies of Rich. He even passed sentence without giving More the chance to argue against the conviction.

Most historians are of the opinion Rich committed nothing short of perjury in the trial of More. Nevertheless, he – and Audley – was well rewarded. Rich gained many more positions of high office. One of his most profitable appointments was as Chancellor of the Court of Augmentations, which gave him the job of overseeing the Dissolution of the Monasteries. It made him a very wealthy man. He had the authority to do what he liked with Church property that the Crown no longer wanted. As a result, he became the owner of more than 100 manors in Essex, including Leez Priory,

Leez Priory, one of the many homes of Richard Rich, who lived up to his name following the Dissolution of the Monasteries.

near Felsted, where he set about building a huge mansion that would be his principal home for the rest of his life. Historian Thomas Fuller famously wrote that when the abbey lands passed through the hands of Rich, they stuck to his fingers!

Audley also benefited hugely from the Dissolution of the Monasteries, gaining lots of land too, including St Botolph's Priory in Colchester and Walden Abbey – his grandson Thomas Howard, 1st Earl of Suffolk, building the famous Audley End House on the site of the latter. Fuller, remarking on the tomb of Audley at Saffron Walden, wrote: 'The stone is not harder, nor the marble blacker, than the heart of him who lies beneath.'

It seems Rich got richer as the years went on. Many accusations of corruption were laid upon him in his position of treasurer of the French wars. Even the King questioned his accounts and is believed to have forced him to resign from the post because things did not add up.

Rich also assisted the Bishop of London, Edmund Bonner, in his relentless persecution of Protestant heretics. In 1546, Rich and the current Lord Chancellor, Thomas Wriothesley, were personally involved in the torture of Anne Askew before her execution, something famous martyrologist John Foxe remarked Rich took much delight in doing. The victim – the only woman on record to have been tortured in the Tower of London – claimed herself that they 'took pains to rack me with their own hands'.

Not long after, Rich received the title Baron Rich of Leez and became Lord Chancellor, but his reputation for treachery grew and he only held the latter post for a few years. However, while others fell with the passing of various political and religious regimes, many losing their lives, Rich survived and prospered. Despite supporting Protestant Lady Jane Grey, he had no problem switching his allegiance to Catholic Mary I when she came to the throne. He also served Elizabeth I, a Protestant, but held less power during her reign.

Some claim Rich tried to make amends for his past in his latter years, his charitable works going some way to improving his reputation. One of his more noble acts was the founding of Felsted School in 1564. The sons of Oliver Cromwell became pupils at the now famous seat of learning.

The notorious Richard Rich regained some honour in later life by founding Felsted School.

Rich died at Rochford, where he had one of his many other homes, but was laid to rest in a grand tomb at Felsted. His funeral was a lavish affair, perhaps successfully serving to represent such an extravagant life. He may have been generous at the end, but there is little doubt he was a selfish and cruel man who would stop at nothing in order to advance his own position.

William Calcraft

It is not necessarily for the fact hangman William Calcraft put to death so many people that has made him a real villain of Essex. When capital punishment was once a feature of everyday life – and death – someone had to do it. However, Calcraft, the most notorious executioner of the nineteenth century, did it in a manner that was far from sensitive. Victorian novelist Charles Dickens, who witnessed many public executions, said Calcraft should refrain from telling jokes on the scaffold, playing to the crowd and drinking brandy.

Dickens campaigned vigorously against capital punishment. Public hangings were big events in London and attracted huge audiences, sometimes amounting to tens of thousands of people. It was one of the most popular 'entertainments' of the day. Dickens wrote in a letter to a newspaper in 1849, after witnessing an execution: 'The conduct of the people was so indescribably frightful, that I felt for some time afterwards almost as if I were living in a city of devils.'

At the very least, Dickens demanded that executions should take place behind closed doors. He eventually got his wish. In 1868, Calcraft himself officiated at the last public execution and the first to be held in private. William Calcraft was born at Little Baddow, near Chelmsford, in 1800. He was a cobbler by trade, but started to sell pies in the streets around Newgate Prison. He became well known to staff there and it led to a job flogging juvenile offenders. When the executioner at Newgate died in 1829, Calcraft was appointed his successor. His first hanging of a woman at Newgate was of Esther Hibner, who had been found guilty of murdering a child. Of all crimes, this was perhaps seen as the most heinous and Calcraft was cheered as he appeared in front of the crowd.

Calcraft also carried out executions at other prisons throughout the country. He had a set wage, but would be paid extra for each execution and any floggings. He earned even more money by selling 'souvenirs'. He was allowed to keep the victim's clothes and personal belongings. Sometimes he would sell part of the rope, particularly if the victim had something of a celebrity status. Occasionally Madame Tussaud would buy the clothes for dressing the latest waxwork in her Chamber of Horrors.

Calcraft was one of Britain's longest-serving executioners, but arguably the most incompetent too. He frequently failed to calculate the right length of rope that was required for each job. On occasions he had to rush below the scaffold and pull on the legs of the victim to finish them off.

In the defence of Calcraft, some would argue he was just doing his job and it was not a job many would like. He sometimes had to hang juveniles. However, Calcraft's jocular behaviour did not reveal a man not at ease with his occupation. Of course, it may have been his form of defence, his way of coping with the horrors of the job. However, Calcraft did not appear to be a pleasant man.

Burnham-on-Crouch is all about sailing these days, though that was not the case in the seventeenth and eighteenth centuries.

In 1869, he was summonsed for refusing to come to the aid of his mother who was a pauper in a workhouse at Hatfield Peverel, near Witham. He said he had a brother and sister who should also be ordered to help, and that he had his own family to look after.

It is estimated Calcraft carried out between 400 and 500 executions during his career. Perhaps no-one could fail to have their heart hardened after being at the forefront of so much suffering. Calcraft was forced to retire in 1874, and died some five years later.

The Admiralty

You would not have wanted bandy legs in the seventeenth and eighteenth centuries. If you did have them, it might have been wise to keep looking over your shoulder. Bandy legs were a sure sign that you were a seaman, and therefore a chief target of the notorious press gangs, groups of men set up to find new 'recruits' for the navy.

Essex, with its proximity to London and also the sea, was a hotbed for the sordid business. It is fair to say the navy contained many a villain. The new 'recruits' were often criminals, specifically targeted as a way of cleaning up the streets. Yobs, vagabonds and petty thieves were usually the first to be forced into a secondment at sea. But when wars abroad became more prevalent, extra men were required and the Admiralty started to target skilled labour, particularly experienced sailors. Bandy legs were often the sign that the individual had already spent much time stooping below the low decks of a ship. However, it was not uncommon for people of other occupations to suffer from the condition and many a tailor, who would sit cross-legged on the floor all day, would find themselves at sea, mistaken for an able seaman. Indeed, many an innocent man would be 'pressed' into service, and, in truth, the real criminals were those responsible for the press gangs themselves. It was nothing short of kidnapping. In defence of the Admiralty, they needed more men and the gangs were legal, covered by special warrants, but it was a cruel business operated by ruffians.

Those serving in the press gangs had to be tough, as a certain amount of force was often required to 'persuade' somebody to join the navy. The commanding officer of a press gang was typically a runt of the navy's litter, though certainly not in the physical sense. He would have often been given the role as a punishment for some misdemeanour at sea. The top naval officers would not aspire to do such work. It was done by those who had little chance of advancement in their chosen career, or, in some cases – particularly if they had been 'pressed' into service themselves – *not* necessarily their chosen career!

The practice of forcing people to join the navy reached its peak in the seventeenth and eighteenth centuries. Men were threatened with prison if they did not 'sign up'. However, many chose a safer life behind bars than dare face the many dangers at sea. It meant the navy turned to force as its preferred method of boosting numbers. Some hardened criminals volunteered to join, but most would do anything they could to avoid such a fate. Brawls usually accompanied the press gangs wherever they went, and that led to even more crime. An alternative escape route was bribery and the wealthy could usually 'persuade' the commanding officer of the press gang that he would be of no use at sea.

The Admiralty would often set up a base in towns, which was given the name 'Rendezvous' or 'Rondy', as they became known.

It was a sort of recruitment office, but also acted as a temporary prison for the unfortunate that had already been 'pressed'. It meant that not even those living in the inland towns of Essex were safe from the press gangs. Inns were chief targets as many a 'recruit' would often be so under the influence of alcohol, the first he knew of his secondment was when he woke in Rondy the next day. Sometimes the undercover press gang officers would deliberately get their targets drunk.

However, it was not surprising that the county's residents most at risk were those beside the coast and particularly the seafarers. Floating press gangs operated along the Thames Estuary, in particular. Ships that tried to outrun the press gang vessels usually received a shot that ripped away their rigging. The Admiralty even had the cheek to charge the captain for every shot it needed to get him to stop his boat. Once aboard the ship, the press gang would order the crew to line up and select the most able-bodied. It was amazing – no doubt – just how many ships had so many 'infirm' crew members!

There was little escape from the clutches of the press gang, unless you were fortunate to have been issued with a 'protection'. This was a much sought-after pass that meant the individual could not be 'pressed' into service. Not surprisingly, bribery was rife and passes were issued liberally by the less scrupulous and by now very wealthy Admiralty clerks!

Such was the fear of a floating press gang lying in wait in one of the Essex estuaries, captains of ships returning from sea, it has been reported, would even go to the trouble of docking at Harwich and swapping their entire crew for a collection of lame men or those that had 'protection' passes. Some might think that was going a little bit too far, but it was better to be safe than sorry. You can imagine what it must have felt like to be a sailor returning after sometimes years at sea, with your home in sight, only to be 'kidnapped' by a press gang and set to sea for another few years. It has been said that criminals along the Essex and Kent coastline on the Thames Estuary, had more chance of being apprehended by the press gangs than by the law.

It may be true to say that many Essex villains deserved to face their fate at sea, but many innocent people were 'pressed' into service and some were torn from their families, never to see them again.

William Kempe

It is perhaps a little unfair to label William Kempe a villain. However, his actions, according to legend, indirectly led to the murder of an innocent child.

Kempe was the owner of Spains Hall in the much-photographed village of Finchingfield, north of Braintree, in the first part of the seventeenth century. The eccentric voluntarily punished himself for having the audacity to accuse his wife of adultery during a fit of rage. In penitence for his harsh words, he vowed he would not utter another syllable for seven years. Even after his wife died in 1623, he kept his promise – but with tragic consequences.

One day, Kempe and his servant were caught in a storm and took shelter among the ruins of a castle. The former soon realised they were not alone. Kempe could hear a gang of bandits plotting to rob a house – his own. It appears the servant had not heard the actual plan and Kempe attempted to use sign language to inform him that the household was in danger. Because they had to reach Spains Hall by crossing a swollen river, the servant graciously offered to swim across it while Kempe took the longer route. Still refusing to speak,

The actions of the eccentric William Kempe are still much talked about in the pretty village of Finchingfield.

Kempe wrote a message on a piece of paper to warn the household of the imminent danger. Sadly, by the time the servant reached the house, the paper was sodden and nobody could read the message. Realising there was something amiss, however, the servant and all the men at Spains Hall rushed off to look for Kempe, the one thing the owner of the mansion did not want them to do. The property was left unguarded and during this time the robbers arrived. They stripped the house of its valuables and, in the process, killed a young boy who had been cowering in the corner of one of the rooms. It is thought he was a distant relative of the Kempes.

It is said Kempe never learned his lesson. Even after this tragedy, he refused to speak. According to some, he actually died just as his seven years of penance were up. Some even say he collapsed when he tried to talk, as, by now, he was no longer physically capable of uttering a single word or sound.

Of course, the tale of the pious William Kempe might have become a little distorted over time and it is difficult to know how much is truth and fiction. As for the young murder victim, it is said the boy's cries can still be heard at Spains Hall on particularly stormy nights.

Ghosts

There are some Essex residents who apparently get up to mischief even after death. Tales of wailing and shrieking ghosts are plentiful, and the county was also once home to the most haunted house in England.

Of course, not all ghosts are said to be bad and many were themselves actually the victim in life, rather than the villain. Now unable to rest in peace, for whatever reason, the county's bad boys and girls from beyond the grave have left unsuspecting residents in all corners of Essex scared witless.

Where better to start a round up of ghostly encounters than at Borley Rectory – once regarded as the most haunted residence in the country before it was mysteriously destroyed by fire in the late 1930s. Ironically, some even believed its resident ghosts had been responsible for tipping over an oil lamp that led to the blaze.

The house was built in the early 1860s, supposedly on the site of a former monastery. Its most famous ghostly tale is of a monk that eloped with a nun from a nearby convent. The couple fled in a coach, but were pursued and caught. Their punishment was severe. The monk was executed and the nun bricked up alive in the convent walls. Needless to say, the lovers – and their phantom coach – have been sighted on many occasions since.

Borley Rectory and its paranormal activities came under the national spotlight in the 1920s. It is said the house inspired more books to be written on physical research than any other place in the world. The church at Borley – a village in the very north of the county – is supposed to be haunted too.

Old buildings, for obvious reasons, have more than their fair share of ghost stories, and you cannot get much older than the chapel of St Peter-on-the-Wall, in the village of Bradwell-on-Sea. It was built in the seventh century when St Cedd landed on the Essex coast and is one of the oldest churches in England. St Cedd built the chapel using stones from the ruined Roman fort of Othona that once stood at this remote location beside the sea. There have been sightings of a centurion keeping watch and

The isolated chapel at Bradwell-on-Sea has had its fair share of unwanted residents, according to legend.

of a cavalryman emerging at full speed on his horse from nearby Mersea Island, once home to another Roman settlement. The sound of galloping hoofbeats have been heard, the Roman said to be warning the garrison of an imminent attack.

Mysterious lights have also been spotted coming from the chapel windows over the years, though many have put that down to smugglers who were known to have hidden their contraband within its walls.

With spectral tales already rife, it is quite probable they used this to their advantage, superstitious locals keeping well away.

Mersea Island is also apparently home to another centurion. His marching footsteps have been heard along The Strood, the causeway that links the island with the mainland. Author Sabine Baring-Gould, who lived at East Mersea, also wrote about the Viking spirits who inhabited Barrow Hill.

Ghosts are said to be the spirits of the deceased unable to rest in peace. The spirit of a former servant at Runwell Hall, near Wickford, certainly fits that description. The house once belonged to Susan Clarencieux, *née* White. She served as lady in waiting to Mary I, and was given the property by the Queen, along with an emerald necklace that the Tudor monarch had received from her husband, Philip II of Spain. George White, the nephew of Susan, inherited the manor, but is said to have stolen the necklace, putting the blame on a servant at the hall. The unfortunate servant was hanged, but, while on the scaffold, he claimed he knew who really took the necklace and added that he also knew where it was hidden. He declared that if ever the thief attempted to get it, he would haunt him forever. Some Runwell folk still believe the emeralds remain hidden.

If you go down to the woods in Thundersley today, you might get a big surprise. Blood-curdling screams were once heard from a copse where it was said a woodsman killed a young boy working with him. In a fit of rage, annoyed by the youngster's apparent laziness, he swung his axe and struck off his head. He hid the boy's torso in a hollow of a tree and told people that the little rascal had run away. However, it appears the young victim wanted everyone to know the truth. It is said his ghost sat on a gate at the entrance of the wood and screamed when anyone approached. The guilt-ridden woodsman turned to drink and eventually confessed his crime at a local pub, and only then, it is said, did the screams stop. For many years, the wood was known as 'Shrieking Boy's Wood' or something similar.

The Sutton Arms pub in Little Hallingbury, close to the Hertfordshire border, was named after the family that produced Thomas Sutton, founder of Charterhouse School. However, another member of the clan was not so celebrated. There is a legend that one of the Suttons fell for a pretty maid who worked at the pub. When she rejected him, he murdered her. It is not his victim that is said to now haunt the property, however, but her remorseful murderer, supposedly intent on making amends.

Another murder victim seemingly unable to rest in peace is Alice Miller. It is said she was killed at the Red Lion Hotel in Colchester in the 1630s. Alice was a servant who lived in the property and is said to have had her throat cut by her own lover, who could not bear to live with the scandal after she fell pregnant. Guests have claimed, among other things, to have heard footsteps from supposedly empty rooms. There are many versions of the story, and some say that Alice actually committed suicide, possibly after committing incest with her own father.

Lady Alice Mildmay, wife of Sir Henry of Great Graces in Little Baddow, near Chelmsford, took her own life in the first half of the seventeenth century, drowning herself in a nearby brook. It was said her husband treated her unkindly. Alice is said to haunt Grace's Walk, a path that runs from the house to Sandon Brook.

The most famous haunted pub in Essex is probably St Anne's Castle at Great Leighs, south of Braintree, which is reputed to be the oldest licensed inn in England. Pilgrims on the way to Canterbury to visit the tomb of Thomas à Becket took shelter there. Much later, it is said the spirit of a local witch also took up residence after her nearby grave was disturbed. Many strange happenings have been reported at the pub over the years, from ghostly sightings to flying cutlery.

Ghosts can certainly be physical. A woman in white is said to haunt the ruins of Hadleigh Castle. A milkmaid named Sally felt the full force of her long ago. Sally bumped into the mischievous spirit one day and was ordered to return after dark.

Not surprisingly, the frightened girl did not obey. However, when she happened to meet the woman in white the next day, the ghost was none too pleased and cuffed the maid so hard, it almost dislocated her neck. From that day, she was known as 'wry-neck Sal'.

There is an interesting ghost story attached to Hill Hall at Theydon Mount, near Epping. It is said seven brothers died there on the same day, more than 300 years ago. They did not approve of their only sister's latest love of her life. The man in question killed each brother in seven duels, one after the other. It is said the sister, full of regret, put on a bridal gown and committed suicide. Another

Hadleigh Castle was once the haunt of a rather violent woman.

version of the tale is that the woman was not the sister of the seven brothers, but actually the focus of their attention and, when she was unable to decide which one to marry, ordered all seven to fight to the death for the right to wed her. Whatever the story, the outcome appears to have been the same, and the remorseful bride-to-be haunted the house and grounds for many years.

Essex also has its share of famous ghosts. Anne Boleyn is said to haunt Rochford Hall, her childhood home, and New Hall, Boreham, where Henry VIII courted her. Witchfinder General Matthew Hopkins reputedly still frequents a number of pubs in Mistley and Manningtree. Sightings of Dick Turpin in establishments throughout Epping Forest have been reported, while the ghost of Lady Emma Hamilton, lover of Lord Nelson, was frequently spotted at the Three Cups, Harwich, where the couple lodged on occasions. Lady Catherine Grey, sister of Lady Jane, is said to haunt Ingatestone Hall, where she spent time in the custody of Sir William Petre.

Not far from Tiptree, it is not a case of the ghost of 'Marley', but the ghost of Marney! The first Lord Marney of Layer Marney Tower died in 1523, before work on his impressive home was completed. However, it is said he now voices his dissatisfaction over

The builder of Layer Marney Tower still makes his presence felt.

the fact the building was not finished to his liking.

Finally, it seems that even ghosts still think about money and wealth. The spirit of the infamous Bishop Edmund Bonner, who became known as 'Bloody Bonner' for his persecution of heretics, now haunts Copford Green, near Colchester, and particularly the parish church where it is thought he was buried. Nearby Copford Hall was once a private residence of the bishops of London. It is said Bonner, fearful that reformers might seize valuable church ornaments, hid the most precious treasures. He presumably never got the chance to retrieve them in life and has since been spotted still searching for the long-lost silverware.

Old Nick

There can be no bigger villain than Old Nick himself. The Devil has been carrying out his mischief in Essex for centuries. In fact, some folk once believed he even had a house in the county. Bleak Wallasea Island, particularly on a dismal winter's day, might be viewed as the ideal location for the Evil One. It is a place where the imagination can run riot. There is an old legend that claims the Devil built a house on the island. He hurled a beam in the air and ordered his workmen to start building on the spot where it landed. Indeed, there was once a property on Wallasea Island called the 'Devil's House'. At one stage it was the only house on the island and it must have been a lonely existence for whoever resided there. One of its former residents was supposedly a notorious witch, while others claim it was indeed inhabited by a demon of some sort, and many chilling stories emanated from within its walls. The house no longer exists.

One of the first recorded appearances of the Devil in Essex, took place in the village of Danbury at the beginning of the fifteenth century. The parish church stands on top of a hill — one of the highest in Essex — and can be seen for miles. Perhaps that was why Old Nick was attracted to it. It was evensong and a storm raged outside the church when the Evil One entered. It was said the Devil, in the disguise of

It is said Old Nick lived up to his name and stole one of the church bells at Danbury.

a friar, wreaked havoc, filling the congregation with terror. The thunder cracked and lightning flashed outside, as the intruder ran amok inside the building. Much of the church was destroyed by the storm, though it appears the superstitious locals, for many years afterwards, blamed the mysterious friar for the damage.

Old Nick must have enjoyed his time at Danbury, as he returned on another occasion. This time he stole one of the church bells. The Devil is said to have a hatred of bells, as traditionally they were sounded to mark the passing of a soul. It was hoped that the noise would scare the Evil One away in order to allow the departing spirit to find its way to Heaven. Indeed, the bell the Devil was blamed for stealing from Danbury was the one usually tolled following the death of a parishioner.

Tradition has it that Old Nick dropped the bell as he made his escape. The place where it landed is now known as Bellhill Wood. The bell was never recovered. Of course, cynics will say it was probably scrap iron merchants who stole it from the church. They may have decided to hide it in the wood, but were unable to return to recover it for some reason. Or perhaps they did? But if anyone spots a large bell in a Danbury wood …

There are many tales of the Devil causing havoc in Essex churches. Old Nick particularly liked to hamper the building of churches, according to legend. However, it was not just churches that he did not like to see built. There are many versions of a legend surrounding the building of a big house at Tolleshunt Knights, near Tiptree, known as Barn Hall. It was recorded that a medieval knight or lord wanted to build a property in 'Devil's Wood', but every night, the Devil tore down what the builders had constructed. Old Nick was said to be furious the lord had the audacity to build his home in his wood. The lord was not deterred and had the courage to challenge the Devil. However, the Evil One picked up one of the beams and threw it to a nearby hill and demanded that his mansion be built there instead. Needless to say, he got his own way.

As for the brave lord, some of the versions say he was killed on the spot or at the very least cursed. The Devil said he would also return for his soul, whether he was buried inside or outside the church. To thwart Old Nick, the lord was eventually buried underneath the wall of the church, neither outside nor inside. This type of burial was, in fact, quite common, parishioners believing it was a sure way of preventing the Devil from obtaining the soul of the deceased.

Old Nick would not miss an opportunity to claim the soul of an Essex resident, as another old legend informs us. Stansgate Priory, near Steeple, north of Southminster, was built on the banks of the River Blackwater in the twelfth century. It no longer stands, though it provided a lucky escape route for a rather reckless ploughman on one occasion. The man was finding his work tough and, in a fit of despair, cried out that the Devil could have his soul if he finished the ploughing for him. Old Nick took him at his word and appeared before him, taking the plough and completing the work himself. The terrified man headed for sanctuary in the priory church. The Devil, against all the rules, followed him into the sacred building. It is said the man eventually escaped from his clutches, though his pursuer's claws left marks on the stone walls. For a long time, the field was known as 'Devil's Field', and it is said it was not ploughed for many a year afterwards, successive farmers too fearful they may receive a visit from Essex's most cunning resident.

Chapter Ten

Hero or Villain?

Even a hero can be a villain. Time can sometimes distort the truth, and many 'great' Britons have (fortunately for them) seen their achievements overshadow perhaps other less than honourable actions during their lifetime.

In doing good for some, others have sometimes suffered as a consequence. It sometimes just depends on which side of the fence you sit as to whether somebody is a hero... or villain.

Queen Boudicca

Few people in Britain grow up without learning about the heroism of Queen Boudicca. Her tale has been retold over and over again in classrooms throughout the width and breadth of the country. Over time, she has become a real heroine for her courage in standing up to the Romans.

However, there is a darker side to Queen Boudicca. Some have even dared to suggest she was no heroine at all, but a crazed killer who took things too far in her revolt against Roman rule. Certainly, thousands of innocent people are thought to have died indirectly at her hands. Roman historian Tacitus claimed 70,000 Romans were slaughtered when Boudicca and her

A contemporary statue of Queen Boudicca in Colchester, though some believe she may not deserve pride of place in the town.

army rampaged through the south-east, beginning their bloody rebellion in Essex.

The Romans invaded Britain in 43 AD. The chief target was Camulodunum, now known as Colchester. There had been previous Roman invasions, but this time they planned to stay for good. Camulodunum was a settlement established by the British tribe Trinovantes, who were ruled by Cunobelinus, who the Romans referred to as the King of the Britons. Cunobelinus is the Cymbeline of the play penned by William Shakespeare.

The Roman emperor Claudius arrived in Camulodunum as victory was in sight. He only spent about two weeks there, but it was enough time to witness the surrender and submission of several British kings. One of those kings was Prasutagus, the husband of Boudicca and ruler of the Iceni, a tribe of East Anglia.

Camulodunum became the centre of Roman authority and prospered. However, things were to change after the death of Prasutagus. His fortune was supposed to pass jointly to his two daughters and the Romans, though the latter did not keep their part of the bargain, refusing to acknowledge Boudicca and the two princesses of Iceni as the rightful heirs. The Romans seized all the land, as well as treasures from the Icenian dynasty. Not stopping there, they then savagely flogged Boudicca and assaulted her two daughters.

One can perhaps forgive Boudicca for plotting her revenge following this ill-treatment. Honour was at stake and she had no intention of letting the Romans get away with this latest act of savagery. Unlike most of the British kings, including her father, she decided she would not sit back and do nothing.

Boudicca assembled an army, mostly made up of Iceni people, but joined by those from the tribe of Trinovantes, who also still had some scores to settle with the invaders. It was said to be more than 100,000-strong. And strong it was, for the Romans had no answer to it. Driven by fury, Boudicca and her followers rampaged through Camulodunum. There was little resistance, the Romans overwhelmed by the surprise and sheer scale of the attack. There was no time to evacuate women or children. They were brutally slain along with the men. Boudicca and her army showed no mercy.

Colchester Castle was built on the foundations of the Roman Temple of Claudius.

Literally no-one was spared. It is said every Roman she could find was butchered, often by torture. The only resistance was at the Temple of Claudius, the settlement's largest and grandest building. The fact it had been built using money paid in taxes by the Britons probably only vented their anger and it soon fell too. In the end, nothing was left of Camulodunum. The entire city was destroyed.

Boudicca's revolt may have started in Essex, but it soon spread. The Roman cities of St Albans and London were next on the hit list. The burning and looting continued unabated, and more innocent Romans were murdered.

It was Suetonius Paulinus, the Roman Governor of Britain, who eventually ended Boudicca's revolt of 60–61 AD. He had been away from Camulodunum on other business. When news of the rebellion reached him, he and his army marched south and met the rebels. This time it was Boudicca and her followers who were outnumbered. There was only one outcome.

Most say Boudicca's last stand was in the Midlands, but there is also a legend that she committed suicide closer to home. Knowing there was no hope, her work completed, the warrior queen is said to have taken her own life by eating poisonous berries at Ambresbury Banks in Epping Forest. Other locations throughout the country have been suggested, but, in truth, there is little evidence to support any of them.

Boudicca's revolt was one of the most important events in the history of Essex and in Britain. There is no doubt Boudicca and her family were treated horrendously and she probably had the right to fight back to defend her native land. However, some have suggested her butchering of Romans resembled nothing short of genocide.

As for Camulodunum, the Romans were quick to rebuild it and ruled for many more years to come. It became a civilised place and the natives were even treated a little better following Boudicca's uprising, which suggests it might not have been in vain after all.

Camulodunum was the first capital of the new Roman Empire in Britain, and today Colchester is regarded as Britain's oldest town. The Saxons, who came after the Romans, gave it its present name. However, the influence of Rome is still very visible in Colchester, most notably in the sections of Roman walls still standing throughout the town.

Some have suggested Sir Anthony Browne founded Brentwood School to make amends for his dubious past.

Queen Boudicca has gone down in history as the most famous resistor of Roman rule and there was no doubt she was made of strong stuff, but, in another 2,000 years, one can only wonder whether she will be remembered as a true heroine or, in fact, a villain of Essex. Perhaps, as it is today, it will be a bit of both.

Anthony Browne

Sir Anthony Browne left a lasting memorial in Brentwood. He is chiefly remembered as the founder of the famous Brentwood School.

And yet there is still one big black mark in his copybook, as far as some residents of the town are concerned. It is an act that many believe still overshadows his greatest achievement.

Browne played a big part in condemning a local hero to death in 1555.

William Hunter was only a teenager when he was cruelly executed in the town for refusing to recant his religious beliefs.

As the local magistrate, Browne was charged with the task of interrogating Hunter when the latter was caught reading the Scriptures in English, an illegal act at the time. He sent him to the notorious Bishop Edmund Bonner, the last Roman Catholic Bishop of London, who ultimately condemned Hunter to death. Browne was himself present when the 'heretic' was burned at the stake.

The country was in the hands of Mary I, the bigoted and ruthless Catholic who showed no mercy to radical Protestants. Browne was himself a devout follower of Rome and an active persecutor of 'heretics'. He truly believed what he was doing was right.

There is a memorial to Hunter in the high street at Brentwood. A massive elm tree also once grew close to the school, on the actual spot where Hunter was executed, according to legend. It was known as the Martyr's Elm, but has since been replaced with a new tree.

It has been suggested Browne founded Brentwood School a couple of years or so after Hunter's execution to ease his conscience. It is perhaps ironic that the good and bad sides of Sir Anthony Browne are now visible for all to see, two quite different memorials standing almost side-by-side.

Browne was Essex through and through. It is believed he was born at Abbess Roding, north of Chipping Ongar, and died at Weald Hall in 1567, being laid to rest at South Weald Church, near Brentwood.

Tolpuddle Martyrs

The famous Tolpuddle Martyrs, as the name suggests, were treated as heroes of injustice when they were pardoned and offered a new life in Essex.

However, they soon fell out with their new neighbours and it was not long before they voluntarily emigrated to escape the hostility shown towards them.

Sentencing of the six agricultural labourers who dared to form a trade union to improve their working conditions in the Dorset village of Tolpuddle, caused an outcry.

Even though trade unions had, in fact, been legal for some time, the men were found guilty of taking an oath of allegiance to a union, which was against the law, and sentenced to seven years' transportation to Australia in 1834.

The sentence was harsh in the hope that it would act as a deterrent to others and stop the spread of further union activity. However, the general public were horrified and made their feelings known. It resulted in the men being pardoned and brought back home. Not surprisingly, the six gained hero status, attending processions and speaking at public dinners. The public raised funds to establish the men on farms of their own. It was decided to settle them in a part of the country where they could start a new life away from the spotlight. Rural Essex was chosen.

Brothers George and James Loveless, as well as James Brine, were settled at New House Farm, Greensted Green, near Chipping Ongar. Thomas Standfield and son John were given a farm at High Laver, just a few miles away. The remaining 'martyr' – James Hammett – only stayed at New House Farm for a brief spell, choosing to return to Tolpuddle where he lived for another fifty or so years. The remaining five eventually moved to Canada to begin another new life.

After moving to the Essex countryside, the men became far more radical and militant than they had ever been in Dorset. They may have been 'innocent' when arrested all those years ago, but – perhaps now spurred on by the attention and recognition they had gained – they refused to concentrate on farming. The first half of the nineteenth century was an age of reform and the men had soon established a local branch of the Chartist association at Greensted. Meetings were held at New House Farm, but they soon outgrew the building and, much to the disgust of local farmers, were adjourned to a nearby field.

Even the vicar complained. The meetings were held on Sundays and it appears church attendance dropped rapidly as a result. There were soon fears of a local uprising. Even though they remained in Essex for several years, the hostility towards the 'martyrs' eventually became so strong, they were forced to up sticks again, this time emigrating to Ontario when their tenancies were not renewed.

There were some happy times in Essex. James Brine wed the daughter of Thomas Standfield in 1839, the couple marrying at pretty Greensted Church, reputed to be the oldest wooden

A Greensted Green cottage housed some of the Tolpuddle Martyrs.

church in the world. However, in general, Essex gave these national 'celebrities' an unfriendly welcome and eyed them with suspicion, viewing them perhaps more as villains than heroes.

Peter Chamberlen

The nation should be grateful for the lifesaving invention of the Chamberlens – a family of seventeenth-century medical practitioners.

They were responsible for inventing the obstetric forceps, an important tool in childbirth even today. And yet, during their lives, and for some years after, many women and their babies still continued to die when the forceps could have been put to good use. It is because the Chamberlens were reluctant to reveal the family secret and instead used it for their own financial gain.

It is not really known which member of the Chamberlen clan was responsible for the invention. Peter Chamberlen, who came to live in Essex to escape the frequent hostility he was shown in London, is

The church where Brine was wed.

most often given the credit. However, it is more than likely his uncle, who shared the same name, was the original inventor. Like his uncle, the nephew was a notable medical man during his time – serving both Charles I and Charles II as physician. He was also an eccentric and very argumentative. This particular Chamberlen, following in the footsteps of his fellow family members, fell foul of the London midwives, suggesting they were incompetent. He wanted to set up a college of midwifery, with himself as the governor. In retaliation, the midwives accused him of having no experience in the matter and claimed his only knowledge of the subject had been obtained by reading books. The Chamberlens were mostly physicians and often criticised for involving themselves in midwifery. It was considered to be the realm of surgeons and only they were deemed skilled enough to deal with problematic births.

However, the Chamberlens' success in the field earned them a reputation, and rumours abounded that they were in possession of a secret instrument to aid them. Despite the family's early forceps being rather crude, there is little doubt they worked.

Peter Chamberlen, who was born in 1601, may have had ample opportunity to put the family invention to good use. It is recorded that he had fourteen sons and four daughters, as well as sixty-five grandchildren. The forceps should perhaps have been put to good use throughout the country too. Giving birth was still a risky business and many died in the process. However, they did not become available for general use. The Chamberlens only offered their forceps to those that could afford to pay a high price for the privilege of having them at hand if necessary. They remained a close-guarded secret, and the Chamberlens would arrive at a location with the forceps hidden away in a box. It is believed one of the conditions of use also involved the woman being blindfolded, though as the forceps resembled an instrument of torture, that might not have necessarily been a bad thing!

Chamberlen died in 1683, but his forceps still did not come to the aid of women universally. His instruments were left to gather dust in the attic of his home in Woodham Mortimer, near Maldon. They were discovered under the floorboards in 1813 and only then offered for general use, though, by then, forceps were already widely in circulation. In fact, some forceps were also being used abroad in the

The former home of Peter Chamberlen – an inventor reluctant to share his secret.

The plaque commemorating Peter and Hugh Chamberlen.

early eighteenth century. It is believed Chamberlen's son – Hugh – travelled to Europe while his father was still alive to sell the family secret, presumably with his approval. To be fair to the Chamberlens, they had also earlier offered to reveal the secret of their success in England, but only on their terms. For whatever reason – probably because they had so many enemies – the offer was refused.

Chamberlen made his home at Woodham Mortimer Hall during the mid-seventeenth century. Like many members of his family, he was ahead of his time. His views were often radical and he was expelled from the College of Physicians for going too far in 1649.

Perhaps Peter Chamberlen should have been hailed a hero, but maybe his own actions are the reason even today many people in the vicinity are unaware that a member of a family of medical pioneers lies in the churchyard at Woodham Mortimer.

Robert the Bruce

It may come as a surprise to find the famous King of Scotland in a book on Essex villains. Of course, he will always be a hero to many for leading the Scots to victory against the English at the Battle of Bannockburn in 1314. That momentous event north of the border paved the way for Scottish independence.

However, to the English, Robert the Bruce was certainly a villain, and there is a strong claim that he was actually born in England – Essex to be precise.

There are certainly a number of documents to support the theory. The Anglo-Norman family of Bruce owned estates and property in England, including at Writtle, on the outskirts of Chelmsford. It has been much recorded that the Bruce family obtained the manor of Montpelier via a Norman knight who fought alongside William the Conqueror in 1066. Robert the Bruce, a descendant of that knight, was born in 1274 and it could have been at Writtle.

Edward I, King of England, was a visitor to the area. Writtle College now stands on the site of King John's Palace, a royal hunting lodge built by King John and visited by subsequent monarchs, including Edward. Could the young Robert, then an ally of the English, have even taken part in a hunt with the man who was to become his arch-enemy?

The Bruces were among many who believed they had a right to the throne of Scotland when it became vacant in 1290. Edward I had the difficult job of choosing just one of the many candidates and his choice of John Balliol, who was supported by the powerful Comyn family, did not please the Bruce clan. However, Balliol's reign was short-lived and, following his abdication, Scotland came under the rule of Edward once more.

There were many rebellions against English rule at the end of the thirteenth and beginning of the fourteenth centuries, though Robert the Bruce did little to suggest he would be the man that would ultimately free the Scots. However, the murder in 1306 of John 'The Red' Comyn – now Bruce's main rival to the throne – was the turning point. Bruce is believed to have personally been responsible for the assassination. With Comyn out of the way, he sped to Scone to be crowned the King of Scotland.

Edward I was furious and regarded Bruce as a traitor. The Bruce family estates in England, including Writtle, were confiscated. Edward was not prepared to stand for what he regarded to be an act of treason and fought back. Bruce's own wife and many supporters were taken prisoner, while three of his brothers were executed. The new King of Scotland, who also had many new Scottish enemies following the murder of Comyn, had to flee and live the life of an outlaw. It was during this self-enforced banishment that Bruce, at his lowest ebb, famously drew hope from a persevering spider spinning its web. If at first you don't succeed, try, try and try again.

And so the royal fugitive did just that – assembling an army in anticipation of seeing off the English for good. Edward I died in 1307, and Bruce was helped by the fact that Edward II was a feeble and incompetent monarch. However, it was several years before the Scots had their day. In 1314, the English army marched north in an attempt to relieve the besieged Stirling Castle, resulting in the Battle of Bannockburn, which the Scots won. However, it was not until the Treaty of Northampton in 1328 that Scottish independence from England was finally confirmed, the new King of England, Edward III, at last recognising Robert the Bruce as King of Scotland and also abandoning English claims of over-lordship.

The birthplace of Robert the Bruce will always be disputed. Montpelier's Farm still stands on Margaretting Road at Writtle. If this is indeed the site of the home where he came into the world, it is perhaps ironic that one of the most famous villains of England was, in fact, an Essex boy.

Montpelier's Farm is a reminder that Robert the Bruce, arch-enemy of England, may have been born in Writtle.

If you enjoyed this book, you may also be interested in...

Haunted Southend
DEE GORDON

The popular seaside resort of Southend-on-Sea has long been a haven for holidaymakers, but the town also harbours some disturbing secrets. Discover the darker side of Southend with this spooky collection of spine-chilling tales from around the town. From ghostly sightings in Hadleigh Castle, to ominous sounds and smells on the seafront, this book is guaranteed to make your blood run cold. Illustrated with over sixty pictures, *Haunted Southend* will delight everyone interested in the paranormal.

978 0 7524 6082 6

Murder & Crime Essex
MARTYN LOCKWOOD

This chilling collection of true stories delves into the villainous deeds that have taken place in Essex during the last 100 years. From the brutal killing of Police Sergeant Eves at Purleigh in 1893; to the murder of a Chief Constable, this book sheds new light on Essex's criminal history. Compiled by a former Inspector with the Essex Police Force and illustrated with a wide range of photographs and archive ephemera drawn from the archive of the Essex Police Museum, *Murder & Crime Essex* is sure to fascinate both residents and visitors alike.

978 0 7524 6083 3

Visit our website and discover thousands of other History Press books.

www.thehistorypress.co.uk